Contents

Editor Greg Payne

Design Editor Liz Wright

Origination Sally Robinson

Published by Greenlight Publishing
The Publishing House, 119 Newland Street
Witham, Essex CM8 1WF
Tel: 01376 521900 **Fax:** 01376 521901
mail@greenlightpublishing.co.uk www.greenlightpublishing.co.uk

Printed in Great Britain

ISBN 1 897738 250

Introduction

For more than a thousand years moulded or stamped disc-shaped pieces of lead and pewter carrying a variety of images, numbers, letters and abstract designs passed through the hands of men, women and children living in most parts of Britain. None of the pieces merited the description *coin of the realm*; yet some certainly served as currency, albeit with limited circulation. As to the numerous other uses to which these enigmatic artefacts were put, well that's what I shall explore in the following chapters.

During the past 12 months, and largely through the pages of **Treasure Hunting** magazine, I have invited finders and collectors of what I shall henceforth refer to as leaden tokens and tallies (because the word "leaden" subsumes the several lead-tin alloys from which some pieces were formed) to send me photographs and Internet images of pieces in their possession. Responses came from far and wide, and not only from Britain. It delighted me to learn that there are enthusiasts in Canada, the USA, France, Holland and Germany who share a passion for leaden tokens and tallies matched only by the dedication of detectorists in Kent, Suffolk, Cambridge, Staffordshire and other hot-spots for finds.

When my appeals for images and information spread beyond the magazine's regular readership, I made contact with several paranumismatists, most productively with David Powell of London, who had been swimming in this esoteric backwater long before I dipped in a tentative toe. He very generously shared not only some delightful images of pieces in his collection, but also introduced me to his on-going project to classify the numerous designs he has observed during his extensive researches. The Powell Classification System has greatly influenced the way I think about designs on tokens. I'm sure I shall refer to it many times as this book progresses; and for those who miss interesting features in **Treasure Hunting** because they don't buy it regularly, I will at some stage provide a fully illustrated grid depicting the 32 basic types. I should also mention here that in putting together the illustrations for that page, and for most of the other pages, I was helped not only by fellow detectorists and by David Powell; a number of dealers and private collectors also chipped in with excellent photographs.

The images on many tokens and tallies delight my eye, especially naive depictions of animals and birds that might almost have been created by Pablo Picasso or an imaginative toddler. But what I enjoy more than all else about the subject is researching - in some cases merely speculating on - the uses to which tokens and tallies were put in the past. It has been a surprisingly neglected field of study among academics, numismatists and writers within the detecting fraternity. Archaeologists have found few leaden pieces when exploring strata on the sites of ecclesiastical buildings, castles, DMVs and other locations where specialised uses of tokens and tallies probably occurred during medieval times. That's a pity because if, from a dozen different sites within a dozen provincial counties, we had just a dozen tokens and tallies positively dated by stratified context to 50-year intervals between 1200 and 1700 we would have data against which to compare the ages and suggest the uses of tens of thousands of pieces that detectorists have recovered from non-stratified plough soil in the same counties. In many cases the detectorists' finds have come from fields within the vicinities of archaeological sites of the types mentioned above. From those finds in those places one can draw inferences - well, I certainly have. But I wish we had more archaeological evidence.

The renowned Mitchiner and Skinner papers published in the *British Numismatic Journal*, 1983/4 ("English Tokens" 1425-1672) provide a detailed, illustrated, invaluable record of riverside finds ahead of redevelopment in London. I'd never be without my copies of those journals to refer to; but it has to be said that they deal almost solely with London, and that in the intervening decades since their publication tens of thousands of tokens and tallies have come to light in the provinces. As you'll see from the illustrations in this book, provincial finds can be as eye-catching as London discoveries.

During my researches I ploughed through several erudite works on medieval economics; and on the social and economic relations between medieval landlords and peasants; even one on the social,

Leaden losses. Untold numbers of lead and pewter tokens and tallies like these were lost or discarded in Britain during previous centuries. Who used them... and for what purposes? This book is a quest for at least some of the answers.

Not to scale

Not to scale

economic and spiritual relationship between peasants and the Church in medieval England. My conclusion was that those academics knew nothing about the tokens and tallies that played such important roles in the lives of the people they wrote about. Even more disappointing to me as a lover of English literature was the conclusion, after a prolonged word-search on the Project Gutenberg website, that authors such as Hardy, Dickens, George Elliot, Defoe - all renowned for their "realism" in portrayals of working-class lives - were equally blind to the leaden tokens and tallies in their characters' purses and pockets. Fortunately, some less celebrated authors did record crucial information which is revealed in my text.

But let me return briefly to the illustrations. While you are about to see some delightful finds, I had to reject many more because the images and photographic prints sent in were not up to the standard essential for the printed pages of a book. I appreciate that my set-up for making illustrations (a Fuji Finepix 602Z, a PC with PaintShop Pro and a broadband internet connection) is quite unnecessary for making excellent token and tally finds as a detectorist. Nevertheless it saddens me that some superb finds are missing here. Many others (finds and donations by ordinary members of the public) are not included because they lie hidden from easy viewing in museums that refuse to allow photography unless hefty reproduction fees are paid. I'm grateful that the one or two enlightened museums who gave me free access to their leaden tokens and tallies for photography grasped this opportunity to disseminate knowledge through a populist author, and to publicise their addresses and opening times (see Acknowledgements). I implore my readers to visit those museums.

An excellent book could be written (might one day be written) using as a framework the 32 types in the Powell Classification System; packing the pages with photographs of every token and tally one could lay hands on and grouping them into 32 chapters or sections. I've taken a different approach, in part because there would at present be huge imbalances between the sections of such a book, but also because I think the story of leaden tokens and tallies in use can be told in a more entertaining way if we read it chronologically, reminding ourselves that the complete history of their use in our islands began with the arrival of the Romans, and that they were still intimately bound up with the lives of some people when Queen Victoria ruled. I hope you enjoy the story's unfolding.

Acknowledgements

The applause of readers who enjoyed this book will ring pleasantly in my ears; but before I hear their clapping I want them to catch my own plaudits for people whose help enabled me to complete the typescript and deliver the illustrations to the publisher.

First, my thanks to paranumismatist David Powell whose enthusiasm for leaden tokens and tallies rubbed off on me soon after we had exchanged a few emails and arranged a joint visit to view the British Museum's huge collection. He was most generous with help when I needed illustrations, asking nothing in return but news of detectorists' finds to assist him with his on-going project to classify leaden token types. I hope all detectorists will keep in touch with David in the future and inform him about unknown tokens and tallies yet to come to light.

Next my appreciations to the several forerunners who contributed articles about leaden finds to the pages of **Treasure Hunting** magazine long before I took any interest in the subject. Their words alerted readers and finders to the fascinations of leaden losses. One who merits special acknowledgement is researcher Bob Alvey, deceased, probably the first detectorist to group his finds into categories and, crucially, to tell us about his system in a magazine article.

Then there are the very many **Treasure Hunting** readers (too numerous to name) who sent me illustrations of their finds. A few - Bob Wells, Alan Calver, Mike Mount, Bob Spall, Paul Baylis, Brian Read, Andrew T. Macmillan, Colin Maggs, Stanley Clute, and the one I'm sure to have omitted - did much more, inviting me to their homes to take photographs, or sending images galore on CDs. In every case time, effort and expense were freely given for the sole pleasure of sharing enthusiasm for a neglected and, in our view, most underrated collecting field.

The Cuming Museum, Southwark, London; Gloucester City Museum & Art Gallery; Salisbury & South Wiltshire Museum; and Moyse's Hall Museum, Bury-St-Edmunds merit praise for their liberated attitude towards photography in this age of digital imagery. Please repay their help with illustrations for this book by visiting their establishments and enjoying their displays.

And of course I readily acknowledge the efforts of those hard workers at the publishers' office - Alan, Carole, Danny, Greg, Liz, Sally - on whom I counted to turn raw text and images into the great book you now hold in your hands.

Finally I want to stress that despite all foregoing acknowledgements, the text of this book - every sentence, paragraph, chapter, caption - is my own work. I am solely responsible for any errors and omissions. If you wish to hiss and boo rather than applaud, please aim all brickbats at the author.

Edward Fletcher

A Note on Scale for Paranumismatists

The illustrations for this book came from a variety of sources, and they reached me as photographic prints and as scans. Some correspondents took great care to carefully measure and record the dimensions of each piece; but the overwhelming majority sent their images in celebration of the designs upon them. That has been my approach. None of the pieces shown on these pages is depicted at actual size; most are enlarged to emphasize designs and to show lettering and words on artefacts that are often dark, and very often worn, as clearly as possible.

Chapter 1

In The Beginning

Ancient metal smiths must have noticed lead ore (galena, or lead sulphide) as an unusual silvery speckle within freshly broken boulders of quartz and other rocks. Early hopes of silver riches would have died as quickly as the ore dulled on exposure to air, though some lead ores do contain silver in sufficient quantities to make smelting profitable. Nearly pure molten lead would have flowed as soon as the quartz stones began to roast on an open fire, but the smelters would have quickly realized that lead swords and spearheads blunted and bent far too easily. Nevertheless, lead's other properties made it the ideal material for sling-shot, for loom weights, for fishing net weights, and for moulding watertight containers.

Around 3,000 BC an enterprising Babylonian cast what might be the oldest lead figurine; and by 2,000 BC the Assyrians had fashioned lead writing tablets, while rolled sheets bearing book-length Hittite inscriptions from 700 BC were excavated at Assur. By the time the Ancient Greeks, then the Romans, had finished exploiting lead's many useful properties, coffins, water pipes, roofs, sheathing for ships' timbers, kitchen utensils and numerous small boxes for perfumes and cosmetics were made from lead across the length and breadth of what we now call Europe.

The practice of moulding or stamping official emblems, owners' names, emperors' images, numbers, weights and similar information into small pieces of lead and using them as closures or seals on bales, amphorae and other containers must obviously have flourished as trade and commerce expanded during periods of *Pax Romana*, and probably occurred earlier as the Greeks planted their colonies and international market-places around the Mediterranean. People living in busy ports and major cities saw leaden seals and tallies every day; even county folk probably became accustomed to using them on produce they sent off to markets in cities and towns.

Urban excavations have yielded lead discs within the remains of amphitheatres and other places where crowds congregated. Some have been interpreted as entrance tickets; some as passes allowing holders access to bath-houses and other amenities. However, the majority of lead discs bearing designs or letters that came to light on all manner of sites during the early years of archaeology and museum-stocking were usually classified as *tesserae*, a catch-all word whose meaning included the ticket and pass usage mentioned above, but which also came to be used for any small embossed or moulded piece of metal (square, oblong or round) that clearly was not a coin.

The Romans also employed the word *tesserae* in a number of ways: for the small stone or glass cubes and tiles used to make mosaics; for dice and playing pieces in board games; for things not unlike Victorian calling cards (*tessera hospitalis*); for what we might nowadays call meal tickets (*tesserae frumentariae*); for pieces used as token money given to deserving poor, just as Boy Bishop tokens, discussed in another chapter, were used centuries later (*tesserae nummariae*); and even for the password used by soldiers to mark friend from foe before going into battle (*tessera militaris*).

That last may have been no more than a spoken word, but there is written evidence concerning the use of military *tesserae* in the ways we have been discussing. For example, during the Punic Wars the Romans sent a message to the Carthaginians offering peace or war. With it went two *tesserae*, one bearing the image of a spear; the other with the image of a caduceus as a sign of friendship.

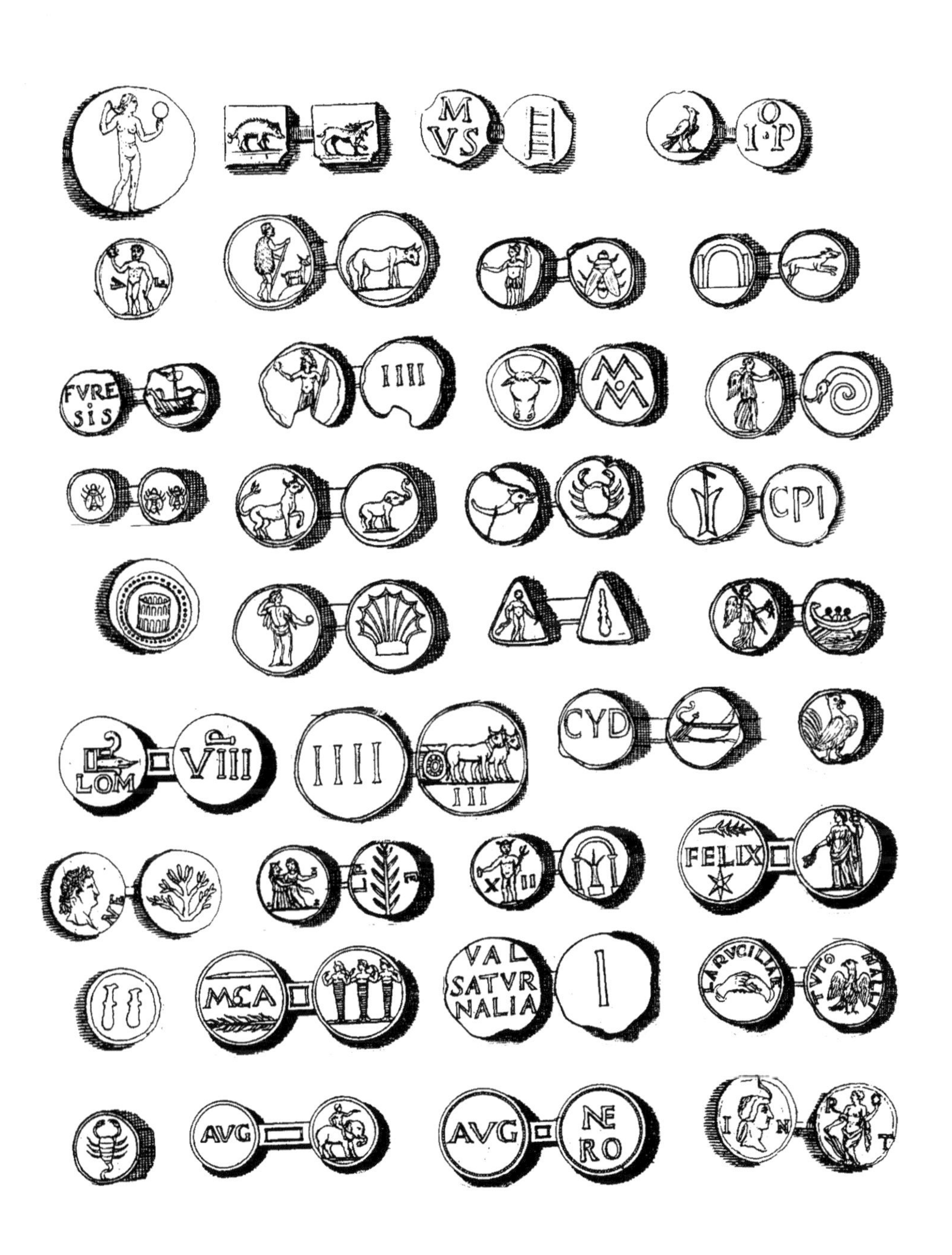

A selection from the thousands of tesserae illustrated in the 18th century work by Francisci Ficoronii.

Not to scale

Perhaps you wonder, as I did, why we seem to know so little about these ubiquitous *tesserae* that pervaded Roman life. Why do we see so few examples displayed in museums replete with Roman coins? I would argue the answer lies in their leaden composition. Upper class (and later middle class) collectors who went on their Grand Tours to Italy and Greece in the 18th and 19th centuries carried with them an attitude of disparagement towards lead. Their interests lay in lavishly decorated pottery, bronze statuary, silver and gold coins. They might have descended as far as large Roman brass to ensure full cabinets in the few public museums back home, but not to the very metal their agricultural labourers clutched as tallies of sweated toil in the fields.

Let us give thanks to the two or three exceptions that always prove rules. First to Francisci Ficoronii, a scholarly Italian who, in 1750, published his **De Plumbeis Antiquorum Numismatibus Tam Sacris, Quam Profanis** at a time when few other antiquarians paid much attention to the subject. Unfortunately, my childhood foothold on Latin's sheer cliff face slipped, so I can't read his entire text in that language. I must rely on his excellent engravings: 40 plates depicting more than 1,000 different *tesserae* illustrating every aspect of Roman life. Emperors, gods, sacrificial altars, senators, benefactors, soldiers, weapons, charioteers, gladiators, heroes, wild beasts, domestic animals, birds, crops, tools, ships, food, amphorae, musical instruments, inscriptions, letters, and numbers - all moulded in humble lead, and a delight to the eye.

Next, Michael Ivanovich Rostovtzeff for his **Leaden Tesserae of Rome And Its Environs**. He published it in 1903 as an account of the ways in which *tesserae* wove into the fabric of the Roman world. In an essay written years after that book he made the comment, "The history of the tessera reflects the whole development and gradual establishment of the Roman Empire."

Alas, M.I. Rostovtzeff's book is also written in a language I have no grasp of (Russian); but fortuitously he provided an index in Latin which anyone equipped with a Collins Gem **Latin-English Pocket Dictionary** can make sense of. Using it I managed to translate more than 90% of Rostovtzeff's classifications. Let me mention some of the leaden token images he found evidence for within Rome and in the countryside around the ancient city.

Nero topped the list among the large numbers bearing busts or names of emperors, with Domitian, Trajan and Hadrian not far behind. Among the panoply of gods and heroes, Fortuna was by far the most popular, with Hercules, either as a figure or represented by his huge club, not far behind. Mars, Mercury, Minerva and Victoria were also profusely represented among more than 60 deities. Of male figures depicted, charioteers, beast fighters, riders, gladiators, young men holding weapons, shepherds with flocks, were all included, while women holding cornucopiae or represented as priestesses were mentioned.

The animal kingdom included eagles, lions, dolphins, deer, ravens, elephants, rhinoceroses, snakes, dogs, scorpions, horses and cocks. Inanimate objects included amphorae, anchors, altars, triumphal arches, caducei, carts, wagons, weapons, shells, crowns, boats, wine flagons, rudders, crescent moons, corn measures, shields and gates. Numerous laurels, flowers and palms ensured the vegetable kingdom was not left out.

The faces of many Roman leaden tokens were given over wholly or in part to numbers and letters. It puzzles me to find the number 5 (V) by far the most common, with 1 (I) a long way behind in second place. The greatest number Rostovtzeff recorded was 22 (XXII). Of the letters, C, CC, CL, CM, DM and X are most common. (They could, of course, be Roman numerals.) Every letter of the alphabet appeared on Roman tokens, often in pairs, very often in threes.

Rostovtzeff's classification of groups who issued tokens included public authorities issuing them for military purposes; public issues for distributions of corn; and public issues for games, venerations, circuses and as gifts. Privately they were issued by guilds, bathhouses, brothels, inns, boat operators, fishermen, pack-horse teams, livestock markets and workshops, to name only some in his index.

I hope that having read the foregoing, you now share my opinion that the average citizen at the lower levels of Roman society was as likely to have leaden tokens and tallies about his/her person as she/he was to have money. And if I now turn to my third exception, let us praise J.G. Milne, an Edwardian numismatist who wrote **The Leaden Token-Coinage Of Egypt Under The Romans**. Milne's argument was not that leaden tokens occurred in Roman Egypt, but that in some parts of the province during certain emperors' reigns, an absence of official coins obliged the locals to make their own leaden substitute coinage. That concept has an important bearing on what I want to say in later chapters, so I feel it important to let you read some of Milne's own words:

"Leaden pieces from various Fayum Towns [excavated before 1900],[are] .. taken to represent a token-money for low values.[...] In my [previous] discussion of these pieces I argued that [some] were probably struck locally at Oxyrhynchus, basing this conclusion on the grounds of the appearance, on the reverse, of the first two letters of the name of the town and, on the obverse, of Athene, the Graeco-Egyptian equivalent of the local deity Thoeris. ...[Others are] greatly superior to those of the first group in

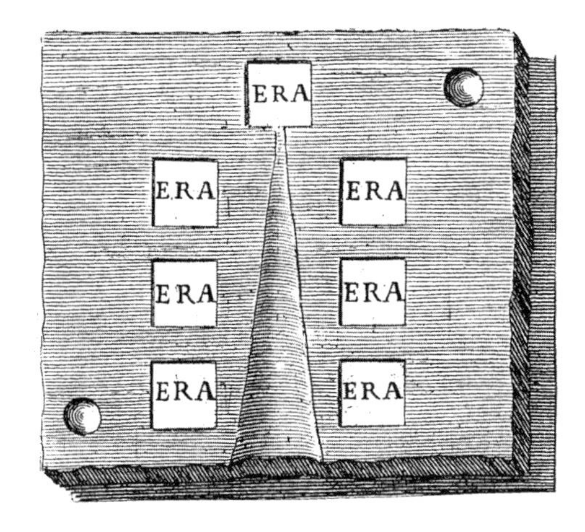

Moulds for casting leaden tesserae.

Lead token coinage from Roman Egypt.

Not to scale

style; the flans are usually round and well-shaped, and in many instances the execution is quite equal to that of the imperial Alexandrian coinage. The types are rather interesting in their relation to that coinage. Many of them have close parallels on the Alexandrian coins, but the treatment of the design, is often varied in some small particular; for example, the usual obverse type of Nilus reclining is very similar to the common representation of him on Alexandrian issues except that on the leaden pieces his figure is shortened to a three-quarter length one, instead of being shown in full. The impression which I have formed from a comparison of this group with the imperial coinage is that the engraver of the dies from which the leaden pieces were struck intentionally altered the treatment of details, while following the general lines of the Alexandrian types; the differences are certainly not due to want of skill on the part of the workmen.

The fact that the pieces belonging to this group only occur sporadically at Behnesa - not more than two examples of any of the types included in it having been found - would suggest that they were not locally struck. The Nilus type is, of course, one which might occur anywhere in Egypt, and it is used, in a style very similar to that of the specimens now under discussion, on leaden pieces which bear the name of Memphis. It would appear that this type was the one most favoured generally in the striking of leaden issues in Egypt, as, out of 137 examples catalogued by Signor Dattari, 68 bear figures of Nilus. [...]

"In my previous article I argued that these pieces represented a local token-currency [...] on the grounds that they were shown by the names upon them to have been struck for certain localities, that they had in some cases a stated denomination, and that they follow for the most part recognized coin-types; and that in the period to which they appear to belong - the latter part of the second and the third centuries - hardly any coins of lower value than tetradrachms were issued by the imperial mint of Alexandria.

"It must be remembered that those coins have all been found singly in the rubbish-heaps of the ancient town, and represent, not hoards of any particular period, but the casual losses of daily life. Unless, therefore, the inhabitants of Oxyrhynchus ceased to drop their money in the streets about 180 A.D., and resumed the habit with greater frequency about 260 A.D. - which seems on the face of it unlikely - some other explanation of the absence of coins of the intervening period must be sought; and it is most reasonable to suppose that the leaden pieces here described, which internal evidence would date to about this time, were in circulation as tokens in Oxyrhynchus, and took the place in daily life, as they do in the rubbish-mounds, of the bronze coinage of earlier years. [...]

"There is not the least evidence that payment in kind or by barter was brought into use; and I know of nothing which has been found in Egypt, other than these leaden pieces, which could take the place. It has been suggested that the imperial coinage of Rome was imported; but Roman silver or bronze coins of before 260 A.D. hardy ever occur in Egypt.

[...] The number of these pieces which come into the market is considerable, but no reliable information can be obtained from the dealers as to where they were found. These instances seem to show that the use of such tokens was spread over the Delta and Middle Egypt, but so far no specimens have been found which can be ascribed to any town south of Panopolis.

Postscript. - [This] ... article was in the printer's hands before the second volume of Dr. Otto's Priest And Temple In Hellenistic Egypt appeared, [in which he suggests] that the Egyptian leaden pieces were [...] tickets entitling the holder to an allowance in kind. If this were the case, however, I should expect to find examples of these tickets of Ptolemaic and early Roman times, since the evidence for the allowances goes back to the second century B.C.; but I know of no leaden pieces from Egypt [...] which could reasonably be dated before the reign of Antoninus Pius. Nor does the general character of the pieces suggest such a purpose as that ascribed to them by Dr. Otto."

Did Roman invaders carry the use of leaden tokens and tallies into Britain? Emphatically yes. Examples have turned up in small numbers almost since metal detecting became a popular hobby in Britain, though many were not recognized as *tesserae* by their finders; in part because leaden objects are generally in poor condition when discovered in arable fields; in equal part because no coin catalogues, almost no museums, and no archaeological reports from 30 years ago mentioned finds of *tesserae*. I offer two possible explanations for the dearth. Firstly most Romano-British archaeological excavations concentrated until quite recently on stone structures such as villas, towns and forts where circulating *tesserae* would have been fewer. Many were probably dropped on rural sites where the peasantry of Roman Britain lived and worked. Few excavations have taken place at such locations.

Secondly the excavators were probably unfamiliar with *tesserae*. They may have classed what looked like fragments of corroded lead as no more than that. It would not surprise me if unrecorded *tesserae* from Romano-British sites lie unrecognised and unpublished in finds boxes and site archives to this day.

A recent series of articles in **Treasure Hunting** magazine about leaden tokens and tallies has alerted readers to the possibility of *tesserae* coming to light. It seems to be having the desired effect; the finding rate has increased from a rare turn-up to an occasional turn-up. It may yet become a steady trickle.

Tesserae from sites throughout the Roman Empire. I suspect that many more await discovery and that some already discovered have yet to be recognized as such

Not to scale

The quality of the engraving of dies and moulds used to make tesserae often matched and sometimes surpassed the engraving seen on Roman coins.

Not to scale

Chapter 2

The Anglo-French Connection

There is no evidence of any lead coinage in Britain during the Roman Occupation, despite Britannia's huge deposits of lead ore, so let us briefly consider what happened to official money as the emperor's grip on the province began to weaken at the beginning of the 5th century.

The upper echelons of Romano-British civil society and the officer class invariably dealt in gold and silver; lowly bronze coins were struck mainly for the convenience of other ranks in the army who used them to buy their everyday needs from natives clustered around camp gates or coming from the countryside to urban markets with produce.

The peasants always faced hefty taxation, and payments were invariably collected in cash or kind; but when payment in kind was unacceptable or inconvenient for the tax gatherers other arrangements had to be made. Perhaps a group of peasants pooled their bronze coins and bought silver and gold at exorbitant exchange rates. Whatever the fiscal mechanisms, they fell apart circa AD 410 when the army crossed to Gaul. Suddenly there was no authority demanding taxes; no market for surplus crops; no need for towns; no requirement for small change. Discarded bronze coins lay thick on the ground along with any now useless *tesserae*. As the Dark Age closed in the economy reverted to barter interspersed with outbreaks of looting and rustling.

Two or three clouded centuries must pass before we have any evidence of a money economy once again established in Britain. As we await the penetrating light let me remind readers that our quest for token usage began with the Romans. We omitted the Celts who had gold, silver and potin money before the Romans arrived. Theirs was a huge nation of loosely federated tribes stretching across much of what we now call France and Britain. Resources - often squabbled over by neighbouring groups - included livestock, agricultural land and ores of gold, silver, copper, tin and the lead already mentioned.

Precious metal coins emblazoned with Celtic interpretations of ancient myths and heroes may have fed the vanities of elites, but they could not meet the essential needs of ordinary Celts going about their day-to-day lives. The Celtic response to that need was an alloy of copper, tin and lead that later historians referred to as "potin", an old French word for pewter. Its most useful characteristic was an extremely low melting point that meant it could be cast over an open fire in simple clay moulds to produce what were in effect pewter tokens. They had little intrinsic value, but by consent of all within each tribe they had an extrinsic value that conveniently allowed them to pass as coins and change for higher denomination coins at an agreed rate. If necessary - for example, when a leader died, or the price of grain rose or the cost of ale and mead fell - the potin pieces could be speedily melted and recast with new images and (possibly) marks of value. The size of potins differed greatly, even between one tribal area and its neighbour, and ranged from 10mm to over 20mm.

The use of potins spread across the Channel from Gaul to Britain not long before the Romans arrived to impose their culture. And the use of coins spread back across the Channel in the 7th century from what, for convenience, I shall now refer to as France, where the first tribal group to rise from the ashes of the Roman Empire and establish a kingdom over a wide area of northern France were the Merovingians. Their wonderful gold coins have come to light in dozens of places around southern England, including the famous Sutton Hoo ship burial site. Less well known are leaden pieces issued by the Merovingians. French tokens experts J. Labrot, and J. Henckes report in their book **Une Histoire Économique Et**

Early Christian lead seals. Their use spread from Rome to France, then to England as the Roman Catholic Church became established here. Leaden tokens and tallies soon followed.

Medieval pilgrim's leaden souvenir found in France.

Not to scale

Populaire Du Moyen Age: Les Jetons Et Les Méreaux that some Merovingian leaden pieces imitated the designs on gold coins, and that an example is preserved in Carnavalet Museum. It shows a cross moline surmounted by a small cross, the same design seen on a Merovingian gold *sous d'or* issued for Paris. Similar leaden finds have come to light on other Merovingian sites. The Merovingian king Clovis the First defeated the last great Roman army in Gaul in 486. Later he became a Christian, as did the kings of subsequent dynasties such as the Carolingians, whose most famous king was Charlemange (768-814). From his reign down to the 13th century the silver *denier*, with occasional half *deniers* (*obols*), were the major denominations, imitated across much of Europe.

Throughout the Continent three important factors played their parts in providing conditions under which leaden tokens once again attained an importance not witnessed since the fall of the Roman Empire.

First, the sapping of the purity and purchasing power of silver *deniers* by constant debasement until most Continental issues became the "black money" so despised by English authorities. Inflation caused the introduction of a double *denier*, then a 4 *denier* coin. By the beginning of the 13th century the value of deniers was hotly disputed between one city and another. Thus in Normandy two *deniers* of Anjou were worth one of Le Mans, while two of Le Mans were needed to buy one English sterling.

Second, the willingness of Continental monarchs to grant local minting rights to barons, towns and monasteries in return for military service, cash bribes or (in the ecclesiastical case) administrative and clerical services. These local devolutions of regal power - almost unknown in England - caused the very economic turmoil and political unrest that made Continental rulers sit so uneasily on their thrones.

Third, the gradual encroachment of the Church into almost every aspect of post-Roman life. Ownership of seals by men of wealth and position had been common in pre-Christian times, so it was inevitable that high functionaries of the Church should adopt the habit as their social and political importance grew from connections with Continental monarchs. The bureaucracies they created became prolific users of lead.

Early in the 6th century they began to attach lead seals to documents to confirm authenticity, or as part of their elaborate archiving systems. One, preserved in the Vatican, dates back to the pontificate of John III (560-573), while a lead seal of Pope Adeodatus I, who was consecrated in 615, depicts on its obverse a shepherd, some sheep and the Greek letters Alpha and Omega; the reverse has the words *Deusdedit Papæ*. The practice rapidly devolved to bishops and abbots, then to cathedrals and monasteries, then to city and town corporations who also frequently used hempen strings to attach small pieces of lead to all manner of official documents.

In her book **Communion Tokens: Their History and Use**, Mary M. Tenney argues that the use of *tesserae* by the Romans and Greeks paved the way for the introduction of tokens into the early Christian Church as a safeguard against traitors and informers in times of persecution; also that the possession of a token helped one of the faithful to recognise another. She quotes Revelation 2, 17 as supporting evidence: "To him that overcometh will I give him a white stone, and in the stone a new name written, which no man knoweth saving he that receiveth it."

Control is a function of all bureaucracies, so it should not surprise us that ecclesiastical authorities soon adapted Roman *tesserae* as a method of recording, and thus controlling, the number of official duties performed by junior priests and others at lower levels of the hierarchy. Early monastic groups often followed the rules of Saint Benedict drawn up in the 6th century, which decreed that monks were to divide each day between agricultural labours, alms-giving, hospitality and prayers, with each activity followed by a brief period of sleep. The times of prayer were fixed and known as canonical hours, and every monk was obliged to observe seven canons during 24 hours. Over time the lives of the secular clergy and of the general population became governed by these times of prayer. Furthermore, leaden tokens were handed out to clergymen during the observances; any priest or monk who failed to attend when under obligation would have found himself short of the necessary tokens that qualified him for the benefits of belonging to the order. The extension of this system to one that controlled all lay persons who served the establishment as farm labourers must surely be the origin of the agricultural tallies used on many British farms until quite recent times.

According to Mary M. Tenney (op.cit.) the first documentary reference to such tokens - in French they are known as *mereaux* - dates from 1375, when Charles V of France granted to the canons of the collegiate church of Langeac, the right to have *mereaux* struck at the Royal Mint for distribution to clerks and canons present at canonical offices. The *mereaux* "were to be of copper, tin, or lead, and to be carefully distinguished by their types, from the coin of the realm." However, Labrot, and Henckes (op.cit.) cite two documentary references from earlier dates: at the church of St Potin, Lyon there were lead pieces bearing the inscription *Moneta Sci Ph* (Money of St Potin) in the 13th century; and at Nevers there was a reference to *merellus* as early as 1167. Whatever the date of their introduction, the use of *mereaux* spread rapidly throughout France and became ever more complex. Rival groups of bishops and canons issued

All of these tokens and tallies came from arable fields in northern France. They would not look out of place in the finds bag of any English fieldwalker equipped with a metal detector.

This English find came from a spot very close to a religious house with strong links to a mother establishment in France. It may be a variation on the French deniers de billon mentioned in the text.

Not to scale

various denominations of *mereaux* in lead and in low-grade silver. These pieces were known as *deniers de billon*, and were probably the forerunners of Continental black money.

Thanks once again to a French researcher, J.A. Blanchet and his **Nouveau Manuel De Numismsatique Du Moyen Age Et Moderne**, we have accurate dates for the introduction and use throughout France of leaden pilgrims' tokens. In the year 1200 a letter written by Pope Innocent III granted to the canons of St. Peter's, Rome the monopoly of casting and selling those "signs of lead or pewter impressed with the image of the Apostles Peter and Paul with which those who visit their thresholds [limina] adorn themselves for the increase of their own devotion and in testimony of the journey which they have accomplished". The pope's language implied that this custom had existed even before he granted the Eternal City its monopoly. In fact, during the 12th century, if not earlier, a very general practice grew up at well-known places of pilgrimage, of casting tokens in lead, and sometimes probably in other metals, and selling them to pilgrims as souvenirs. Blanchet described several types (St Martin, St Michel, etc) and listed places in France where they were manufactured and sold, including Paris, Tours and Lyon. (I'll mention here his statement in the same passage that "the seals were also applied to cloth to indicate its source.")

If space permitted, we might return to Labrot, and Henckes (op.cit.) for a detailed account of the origins of East Anglia's renowned Boy Bishop tokens, which we will cover in a later chapter. Similarly, we could read accounts of French researchers telling us that numerous cities and towns in France had guilds, brotherhoods (*confréries*), corporations, tax collectors, charitable offices, toll collectors and other institutions - all using leaden tokens and tallies in early medieval times. Instead, let me briefly mention someone more familiar to my readers: Richard the Lionheart. He ruled here from 1189-1199, and most of us would call him a renowned English king. But the truth is he spent hardly any of his reign in this country; he spoke scarcely any English; he regarded himself and his court as Angevin French; he even died from a crossbow wound while fighting at the gates of Paris. Like monarchs from William I to Henry IV, he treated England very much as a province to which French habits, customs and institutions devolved. The Church felt and behaved in the same way. Almost all the great medieval religious houses had their roots in France and transplanted their rules and orders to England as off-shoots. With them came a prolific use of leaden tokens and tallies.

Let me end this chapter by stating a great difference between modern France and modern England: they have most of the research sources; we have most of the recovered leaden tokens and tallies. Why? Because vast quantities of written records were lost to modern researchers during the English Reformation. The Suppression of Religious Houses Act began in 1535; by 1540, no monasteries or other religious houses remained. All of their assets had been taken for the king; their records scattered to the winds. Leaden tallies and tokens tossed to the ground or into rivers remained hidden until the advent of metal detecting as a hobby. During more than 30 years British metal detectorists and mudlarks have recovered many thousands.

In France, on the other hand, where an almost unbroken line of Roman Catholicism runs from ancient to modern times, volume upon volume of ancient records and manuscripts survived until researchers including those I have quoted began to seek evidence of *mereaux*. Untold numbers of lost and discarded pieces remain to be found in France because the metal detecting hobby, although popular, has relatively few enthusiasts who search on arable land.

Chapter 3

Early English Tokens

William of Normandy celebrated his victory at Senlac by founding a great religious house that became Battle Abbey. But the new king of England did more than raise a stone monument to his military prowess; he (and his successor, William Rufus) also staffed the new abbey with brethren from the Benedictine abbey at Marmoutier in Normandy. Those Black Monks, together with Cluniacs, Premonstratensians, Carthusians, Cistercians and members of several other Continental orders undertook their own colonisation of England during the next couple of centuries and established new cells throughout the land.

Renowned for their agricultural skills, the Benedictines soon had profits flowing in from vast holdings given by rich Normans eager to book passage straight to heaven. The monks' success had much to do with management and organisational skills; they actively encouraged the best Anglo-Saxon peasants to become lay brethren and to act as what in modern parlance we would call foremen, who in turn persuaded lowlier peasants to work on abbey lands in return for generous food allowances and good shelter. All of this gave the fully fledged monks more time to concentrate on religious duties, manuscript copying and charitable works.

Speaking and writing in medieval French and Latin, they and other orders must have followed French and Holy See practices in all things ecclesiastical; if 11th and early 12th century French monks were using *mereaux* to regulate attendance at services and for other purposes, their Anglo-French offshoots must have done likewise, despite the fact that there is almost no English documentary or archaeological evidence for leaden tokens or tallies during the first one and a half centuries of Norman presence. Few extensive searches for leaden tokens have taken place around early abbeys and monasteries anywhere in Britain. We have to rely largely on Mitchiner & Skinner (op.cit) and their detailed account of Thames riverside finds in non-ecclesiastical contexts, and on detectorists' low tide finds between Gravesend and Teddington, to tell us that, based on the occurrence of nearby coin losses, leaden tokens (and perhaps tallies) were in use in London about the year 1200.

As to what they were used for, we can only look at the finds and the images on them and hope that our interpretation of what we see from this distance in time is accurate.

The earliest English finds were made from pewter rather than lead, a fact that is in itself a strong indicator of monkish manufacture because the Church held a tight monopolistic grip on smelting and using pewter until around 1350. Most early pieces had a high tin content, while the very earliest were almost pure tin and moulded with loops for sewing to garments. Images on early pieces included some with obvious religious connotations (mitred bishops, Pascal lambs, the letter "A" probably as the first letter in Ave Maria); and others that might have had contemporary heraldic or emblematic significance now lost to us (birds, floral designs, deer, etc). We can also see that tiny sewn-on types soon gave way to circular tokens approximately the size of our 5p coin, and almost always with a beaded border around what might have been the obverse face that usually carried the more elaborate decoration.

Not long after 1300 changes occurred. The beaded border gave way to a linear border; tokens became thinner and slightly smaller; but the standard of workmanship by whoever carved the moulds remained high, and even in some cases improved.

These sketches plot developments in early English token shapes, sizes, and designs from 1200 to 1400.

Row.1. shows the small sewn-on pieces that appeared around 1200.

Row.2.

Row.3.

Row.4.

Rows. 2, 3, and 4 show early beaded border types and their unbeaded reverses.

Row.5.

Row.6.

Rows. 5 and 6 show pictorial types with linear borders and an increasing number of designs.

Not to scale

Rows. 7 and 8 show later pictorials at a period when standards in mould carving had declined considerably.

Row.9. shows the neat geometric styles that appeared around 1400.

Not to scale

Subjects depicted on tokens included most of the previous designs and added images such as bears, fighting cocks and pilgrims in various poses wearing appropriate costumes and hats, with some carrying staffs holding tied-on bundles. Clearly these pilgrims' tokens had by that time achieved importance. We have already seen (Chapter 2) that pilgrimage had become a source of revenue for the Church in the 12th century.

By the beginning of the 14th there were about 500 monastic establishments in Britain, some claiming to possess religious relics, others located along what became important routes for pilgrims journeying to see or touch sacred objects. No doubt many faithful Christians made perilous journeys to visit Continental shrines; but a more recent focus of attention was Canterbury where the bones of Thomas à Becket, murdered in 1170, had by 1300 become a major attraction that drew pilgrims from both sides of the Channel. Some of the faithful seem to have carried tokens as the equivalent of round-trip tickets that gave them access to hostels run by monks. Buying badges, and perhaps souvenir tokens, also seems to have occurred at many places en route not only to Canterbury, but to shrines at Walsingham, St Albans, Glastonbury, Winchester, Ely and many more.

After 1350 - by which date the whole of Europe had suffered massive population loss as a result of the Black Death of 1348 - other tokens appeared alongside, perhaps in competition with, the pewter issues. The newcomers had less tin in their alloy; some consisted exclusively of lead; sizes also diminished slightly; but the most noticeable difference between older and newer pieces was the standard of mould engraving, which declined considerably. An explanation for increased use of lead might have been a shortage of tin miners in Cornwall. Competition leading to a need to reduce cost and quality might also have come from secular pewterers and other craft-workers in cities and towns who challenged the ecclesiastical token-making monopoly. Poorer pilgrims would surely have welcomed these opportunities to buy cheaper souvenirs.

The closing years of the 14th century witnessed the emergence of smaller, neater lead tokens with geometric designs gradually superseding pewterish pictorial tokens, though circulating alongside them over many years. Perhaps this reflects a more widespread use of tokens for non-religious purposes. These types heralded the introduction in the next century of tokens with remarkably coin-like features. A further hint that tokens might become the equivalent of small change lies in the fact that among the earlier pewter and lead pieces we have discussed in this chapter a few have come to light cut into halves and quarters, mirroring practices with silver pennies.

The tidal foreshores of the River Thames yield early leaden tokens such as these. Similar finds must await discovery throughout Britain wherever a medieval ecclesiastical establishment flourished between 1200-1400.

Not to scale

Proof that other English rivers flowing through ancient cities and towns hold similar losses to those discovered in the Thames comes from finds made when the River Avon in Salisbury was dredged and yielded an impressive assortment of early tokens, pilgrims badges and similar losses and throwaways from the city's medieval past.

Not to scale

Chapter 4

The Boy Bishop Phenomenon

Whenever I look at a Boy Bishop token nowadays it brings to mind a vivid image of the actor Charles Laughton in one of his most famous roles as Quasimodo in the film, "The Hunchback Of Notre Dame". Do you recall that the medieval Parisian mob elected him the "King Of Fools"? They were doing almost the same as the medieval junior clergy of East Anglia did in electing their Boy Bishops. But the English Christian tradition drew on much older practices, the first of them pagan I might add.

To trace this we must go back to Ancient Rome when the city celebrated the Feast of Saturnalia at around what later became Christmas Day. It was a time when all normal rules of Roman society turned upside down. Law courts closed and class distinctions vanished. Slaves became free for a day and were allowed to wear the clothes of their masters who waited on their tables, handed out gifts of money, and hailed as king the slave elected to that throne by his fellows. Numbers of Roman leaden *tesserae* have been found on which the letters IO SAT, abbreviate a salute that translates as "Hail Saturn!" who was god of the winter solstice. Perhaps, like Boy Bishop tokens, the *tesserae* were thrown to Rome's poor as the new king was carried shoulder high through the streets.

J.A. Blanchet (op.cit.) describes medieval French ceremonies as *"known variously in towns and cities as The Feast Of Fools, The Festival Of The Donkey and the St Nicholas Festival.*

Although the Church officially deplored such celebrations, it was obliged to tolerate them; sometimes even high-clergy joined low-clergy and took part in the festivities. For example, at Leon, in the 13th century, the chaplains, the vicars, and the chorus-singers, assembled in the choir of the cathedral after the morning service, to elect a Patriarch of Fools, donating to him and his entourage bread, wine, money to the value of eight livres parisis, as well as items of costume including a mitre and torn church vestments. For two days religious life gave way to processions, buffooneries and parodies of church ceremonies. In some cities and towns the elected patriarch had cardinals called consors. They received lead or tin pieces as attendance tickets, perhaps also for use in games of chance. In memory of the festival, pieces were also distributed to the crowd. Sometimes a special seal was struck to mark the occasion. The Feast of the Innocents, organized by choir-boys, was similar but less scandalous. It commenced during the Saint Nicholas Christmas celebrations, with choir-boys taking the place of canons. A burlesque was followed by a procession through the city, and a banquet for the participants. The Bishop of Innocents also had his own currency. At Laon, the inhabitants met after Christmas to elect a King of Town Criers, who had a constable and his méreaux of lead. The entourage then made a street procession, told jokes and distributed the lead money".

After those descriptions from medieval France it seems scarcely necessary to describe what went on at East Anglian affairs; but there are one or two points in Blanchet worth further discussion. First, he tells us that the ceremonies were *"...known variously in towns and cities"*...[and that] ...*"although the Church officially deplored such celebrations, it was obliged to tolerate them."*

Surely it is highly unlikely that medieval East Anglia alone in England parodied ecclesiastical ceremony? If the higher Church authorities who *deplored such ceremonies* had only East Anglia to deal with they would have acted to suppress them. Mitchiner and Skinner cite *Proceedings Of The Suffolk Institute Of Archaeology (1978)* in which contributor S.E. Rigold wrote on the Boy Bishop cult *"throughout England."* Yet time after time I've been told when admiring Boy Bishop tokens that they were found in the fields of

Boy Bishop token mould. (Photo courtesy Moyse's Hall Museum).

This half of a Boy Bishop mould came to light during a metal detector search in East Anglia.

A Plasticine pressing from the mould clearly shows the bishop's mitre.

Not to scale

Another remarkable find by a detectorist: a strip of Boy Bishops fresh from a mould and with lead sprue still attached.

A photograph from the underside shows that two sizes of Boy Bishop tokens could be cast in the same mould - as obviously occurred with the museum's mould.

Not to scale

East Anglia. Why have they not come from the vicinities of other medieval towns? I can only surmise that the rich agricultural hectares of East Anglia provide numerous opportunities for recoveries during the ploughing season, whereas other towns with medieval histories have few nearby arable fields. Or that their local arable fields have yet to be surveyed with metal detectors.

Second, Blanchet's mention of *lead or tin pieces* chimes sweetly with the evidence of pure lead tokens circulating alongside pieces made from alloys rich in tin in 13th century London. The Black Death ravaged all of Europe and economic consequences, including a steep rise in the price of tin, would have affected the choice of metals for making tokens in France as well as in England.

Third, the comment that, *"They received lead or tin pieces as attendance tickets, perhaps also for use in games of chance"* confirms that leaden attendance tickets were in use in medieval France; it may also throw some light on why many Boy Bishop tokens have coin-like reverses. What better when gambling than to have playing pieces with one face that resembled the contemporary regal coinage? But numismatic evidence gleaned from the designs on pieces so far recovered suggests a date for commencement of Boy Bishop ceremonies in East Anglia as late as the 1480s. Perhaps they took place without leaden tokens in earlier times.

Highly prized by collectors are those lead pieces that have a bishop's bust on the obverse and a reverse design that mimics a groat, with inner and outer rings of lettering, a long cross, and three pellets in each quarter. But where a Henry VII groat reverse had *Posui Deum Adiutorem Meum* and (probably) *Civitas London*, a Boy Bishop groat usually had some reference to *Sancte Nicholoae*. The saint's name also replaced the king's in the obverse.

During the same period (1480-1530) another groat-sized piece (that's about the size of a modern 2p) depicted only the bishop's mitre on its obverse, but still imitated a coin on its reverse. A smaller lead token, perhaps imitating a penny, had a mitre on its obverse, but only an outer legend on its coin-like reverse.

Other pieces have come to light. Experts suggest that those with black-letter inscriptions were made later than the pieces described above - perhaps between 1530-1550. Later still came tokens issued during the reign of catholic Mary Tudor, in whose reign (1553-1558) the Boy Bishop ceremonies were briefly revived. Those pieces usually have no legends.

Enthusiasts who enjoyed **Tokens & Tallies Through The Ages** will recall the superb mould for Boy Bishop tokens on display in the Moyse's Hall Museum, Bury St Edmunds. The photograph from that book is reproduced here alongside a more recent Boy Bishop mould find, made by an East Anglian detectorist. Even if other moulds fail to come to light, I'm sure many more Boy Bishop tokens await discovery, and not only in East Anglia.

Typical no-legend types, thought to date from the reign of Mary Tudor.

These pieces exhibit similarities to some aspects of East Anglian Boy Bishop tokens. They could be later issues ... or earlier issues ... or issues from other areas.

Not to scale

A superb example of an early groat-type Boy Bishop with well struck obverse and reverse showing the full bust and full legends. (Originally from the collection of Ivan Buck.)

Obverse and reverse of another early groat-type with a reverse imitating the sovereign shield style seen on some Henry VII pennies.

Pieces depicting mitre and legend only seem more common than bust types.

Typical long-cross penny reverse types.

Not to scale

Chapter 5

Tokens & Tallies After 1400

In ways that might have altered token and tally usage, how did the England of 1401 differ from the England of 1201? I would argue that life for people at the lowest social levels had changed almost out of recognition.

Serfdom and unwaged peasant status had gone forever in the aftermath of the Black Death. Now the majority of men, women and children sold their labour and paid in cash for food and shelter. The more adventurous had begun to seek their fortunes in towns, or to see the world as carters, drovers, riverboat oarsmen and pack-horse teamsters. The most enterprising had become chapmen, roundsmen, or even shopkeepers and small merchants.

Wool and everything that could be manufactured from it and sold at home and abroad drove the economy. Those goods brought gold for the richest merchants (medieval monarchs usually ranked second only to the Church as wool dealers.) The goods also brought vast quantities of silver coinage, some of it greatly inferior to our own money. Let me briefly explain why.

Pure silver makes poor money. Coins struck from it rapidly wear and lose value, so mints always add small amounts of harder base metal to the melt to improve silver's durability. Thus the weight of a silver coin cannot equal its true bullion value. The percentage of the baser metal added to it must also be known. We can then state the percentage of silver as the coin's purity, otherwise known as its fineness. Back in 1067 William I created a new mint at the Tower of London and decreed that Tower silver's purity would be 925 parts per thousand. This became known as *sterling silver*, and coins were made from silver of this standard right up to the 20th century. During the early medieval centuries English pennies were known throughout Europe as *sterlings*.

Continental wool buyers - princes, bishops, leading merchants with access to mints - copied the designs on English sterlings to ensure acceptance of their money; and some, knowing the perennial shortage of halfpennies and farthings in England, produced copies of sterlings containing a half or a quarter of the silver. These copies, soon referred to as esterlings, and sometimes called crockards, pollards, eagles, lionines, staldings, or, thanks to their dark colour due to low silver content, "black money", found their way to England in huge numbers, where they circulated in local markets as substitutes for halfpennies and farthings. In some instances when their silver content was fairly high, they could be passed on to the unwary as genuine English money.

The practice grew up of foreign merchants bringing Continental goods to England and insisting on unclipped sterlings in payment; then shipping the sterlings across the Channel and melting them down to produce esterlings. This went on during most reigns. Kings raged against what they saw as bullion smugglers; they passed laws, appointed searchers to check outgoing baggage at ports, made examples of the few they caught. But money smuggling continued.

One monarch who achieved a notable, though temporary, victory was Edward III. In 1335 he issued, with no advance warning, a substantial coinage of halfpennies and farthings at .833 fineness - lower than the equivalent esterlings. The smugglers were unable to offload their foreign money. But English halfpenny and farthing mintings soon dried up. The smugglers were back in business and black money back in circulation.

The same king was, by an Act of 1354, the cause of a massive increase in the number of small pieces of stamped lead passing from one person to another

Developments in English token shapes, sizes, designs from 1400-1500.

Not to scale

Shields and wheel-like designs on small flans appeared in the early 1400s.

Not to scale

throughout much of England. I refer to the Alnage Duty, a tax levied on bales of cloth to which lead seals had to be attached to confirm inspection for size and payment of a few pence in duty. Although monks - still by far the major owners of sheep - probably made many cloth seals, numerous secular hands must also have become experienced at melting and casting lead.

For example:-

In 1394-5 those who paid tax on cloth in York included 39 merchants and mercers, 18 drapers, 12 weavers, 6 tailors, and 3 dyers. Many men and women paid only on very small quantities while others were dealers in a large way. John Braithwaite, a merchant, paid on 134½ cloths; Robert Ward, mercer, on 79; Richard Redehode, draper, on 77¼; Thomas Gare, merchant, on 110½; Thomas Holme, merchant, on 70½; and so on [...]. Some mercantile capitalists were organizing textile production on a putting-out system: the mercer Robert Collinson, who died in 1458, left to the 'dyers, fullers, shearmen and weavers working with me, from whom I have had any goods, a good breakfast and 12d. each'. [...] But it was probably more characteristic for merchants and drapers to buy cloth from independent producers in and around the city and to pay the tax on it when they had it sealed. At the same time, some small producers both of the city and the country also paid tax when they marketed their cloth in York.

From: **The Later Middle Ages: Economy And Industrial Prosperity: A History Of The County Of Yorkshire**.

Let me now mention two or three aspects of medieval life that scarcely altered from one century to the next. The Church continued to pervade almost every facet of social life in 1401. Pilgrims continued to tramp dusty and often dangerous routes to holy shrines in the new century. And despite the fact that many more now had a hammered silver coin or two in a small purse, every man, woman and child who visited a shop or market-place confronted the difficulty of getting change for a penny, and of figuring, or guessing, the silver content of the perplexing array of coins passing from hand-to-hand.

In our 21st century lives many of us become quite annoyed when small coins accumulate in pockets and purses, so let me emphasise the difficulties of living without change. Suppose that I decided to get rid of the junk and clutter presently filling several cupboards and shelves around my home by holding an impromptu garden-gate sale, with numerous items on offer at 10p to 50p each. Suppose also that everyone who stopped to buy had only £1 coins in cash. How could the sale proceed?

One solution would be for me to hand out small cardboard discs, perhaps with my initials on one side, and a value (10p, 20p, 30p, 50p) on the other. Buyers would have to call back at the end of the day, bringing the discs in batches amounting to £1 in value, for which I would hand over a £1 coin. Of course, I'd have to beware strangers when redeeming my discs, ensuring that nobody had made a few counterfeits during the day; but I'd expect most customers to be neighbours and trustworthy. I think I'd take the risk rather than taking barter and ending up with more unwanted items to refill those cupboards and shelves. I might also find that some of my original customers, unable to hang around waiting for the end of my sale, had taken their cardboard discs to another garden-gate sale in the next street and bought items from somebody who trusted my integrity sufficiently to accept the discs and square-up with me later.

Let's look again at River Thames leaden finds, especially at those types Mitchener and Skinner dated by associated coin finds to the 15th century; and at some that might be 15th century losses from the provinces. What happened to tokens and tallies after 1400 given the economic, social, religious changes and continuities in medieval life I have just very briefly sketched?

Late pictorials and geometrics from the previous century continued to circulate, but were joined by new tokens of half their size. Some were made from pure lead and often depicted shields and/or what look like spoked wheels. Accompanying them came pieces in pewter on broader flans and of better workmanship and bearing what might have been merchant marks including ships, utensils, barrels, petals and other devices. A third series also rubbed along with them: larger, thicker tokens in lead (a few in pewter) with images of a poorer standard, and often using stock designs rather than merchant marks. Frequently used emblems on these cruder pieces included petals, grids, wheels and cartoon-like human faces.

Around 1430 large numbers of tokens with one side clearly identifiable as the reverse made their appearance. This reverse mimicked the cross-and-pellet reverse design seen on lower denomination silver coins throughout the 15th century, with the difference that the outer rim of each piece had a border consisting, not of a coin-like legend, but of sloping lines. Obverses repeated the same outer rim design, often using a Gothic letter as the main element where a coin would have had a king's head. As the century progressed the Gothic letter types were joined by other pieces with similar rims, but with merchant marks, wheels, tankards, boats, and other designs in the central obverse position. Beyond London the wide border shrank or was often omitted on pieces that used similar Gothic lettering and merchant marks.

Towards the end of the century a further development saw the return of larger tokens, now made of pewter as often as lead. On many the similarity to coins is even more pronounced, with hints of letters

The symbols on some of these pieces may be merchant marks or elements from guild emblems.

Not to scale

The symbols on some of these pieces may be merchant marks or elements from guild emblems.

Reverse of a genuine hammered silver penny circulating in the 15th century.

Not to scale

where the legend sits on coins, especially on the obverse. Many reverses also continued to display the cross and-pellet design, often with a more elaborate cross. Some of these larger tokens were now given over to human features on the obverse. When letters occurred they were now more likely to be from the English alphabet rather than in Gothic.

A craftsman capable of making bale seals was just as capable of making tokens and tallies, and of appreciating their usefulness. The Church must have faced stiff competition from secular token makers - pewterers and plumbers for example - in the production of cheaper souvenirs for pilgrims, and in supplying the needs of merchants and employers wanting foolproof methods of recording workers' output. The Cornish tin industry, ravaged by the Black Death, seems to have recovered sufficiently to support increased production of pewter tokens towards the end of the century.

Coin imitation hints at the use of tokens as change in busy markets, perhaps in shops and taverns. And London finds from Gravesend to Teddington show that there was a need for tokens on rivers, perhaps as pay tallies given to oarsmen; or perhaps used as change when giving/taking fares on boats and ferries. Farm workers throughout rural England, whether employed by monks or secular landlords, needed pay and change; and they must have wanted just as eagerly to record their daily toils in the fields by accepting leaden chits or tallies. Surely no working man, woman or child in 15th century England failed to come into contact with leaden tokens and tallies at least once a week?

(*o*) The pennies in the following liſt were all found together, under a barn floor, near Newbury in Berkſhire, in the year 1756, and afterwards came into our hands, and are here ſubjoined, as a ſupport to what has been ſaid above, in relation to the plenty of ſome ſorts and ſcarcity of others; being 3520 in number, weighing 155 oz. 15 dwts. or about $21\frac{1}{4}$ Troy grains each penny at a medium.

Berewici	37	Eboraci	58	Lincol.	26	Iriſh	36
Briſtolie	85	Exonie	5	London	1660	Scotch	28
Cantor	1017	Hadelele	6	Novicaſtri	32	Foreign	51
Ceſtrie	3	Kyngeſton	10	Sciedmundi	128	Obliterated	31
Dureme	317						

The Engliſh and Iriſh were all of Edward I. and Edward II. the Scotch were moſtly of Alexander III. and a few of John Baliol; and the foreigners all of them imitations of the type of the Engliſh ſterling; that they might by that means paſs undiſtinguiſhed amongſt them, they being a famous and well known coin †, four of which we have cauſed to be engraven, viz. (A. B. C. D.) of which (A. B.) were coined by the ſame LORD, and at the ſame place, viz. SERAIN, (C) was minted at Aloſt in Flanders, and (D.) at Mons in Hainault. The head ſide of (B.) is like that of the Iriſh Edward, and that of (C.) like the Scotch Alexander III. the money of both thoſe nations running then current with the Engliſh ‡. The legend on the head ſide of (D.) is exactly like that on the Edwards (only AGNL. inſtead of ANGL.) but on the reverſe it has MONETA MONTES, and therefore we may ſuppoſe it one of thoſe counterfeit ſterlings prohibited to be imported at this time §. All the above are of good ſilver, but how much worſe than ſtandard we cannot determine; but more of theſe Coins hereafter.

An 18th century account of a hoard find that included esterlings.

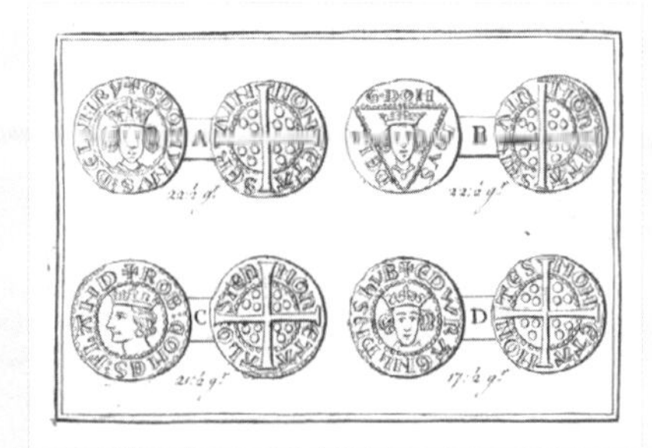

Engravings of the esterlings from the hoard.

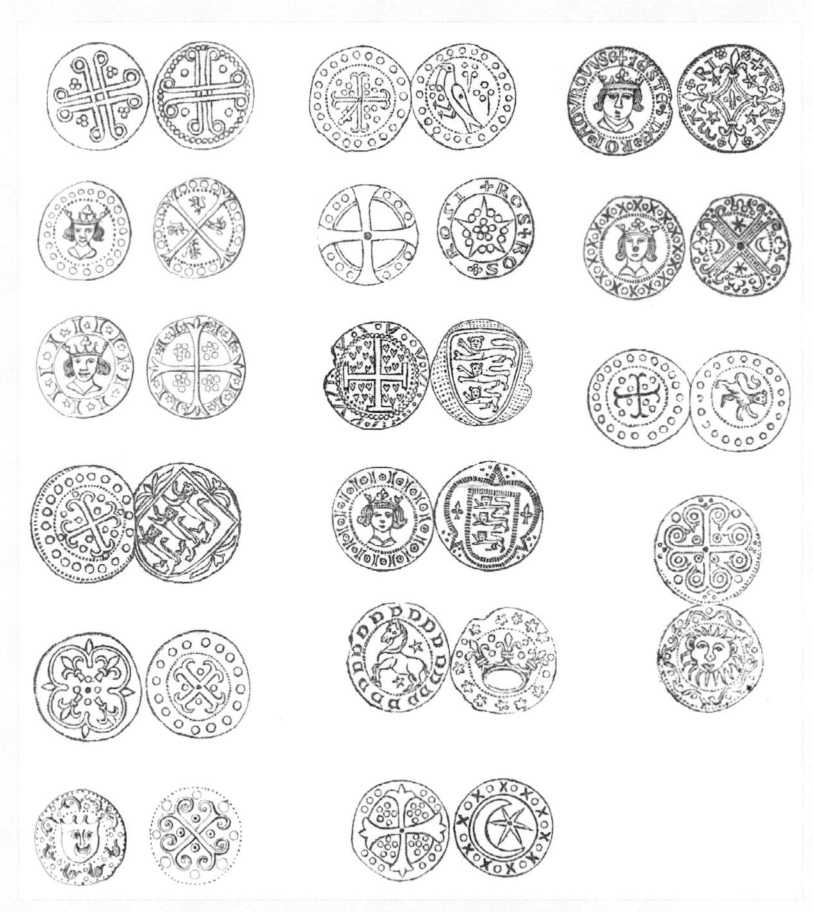

18th century engravings of black money that circulated in England in the 15th century.

An example of black money found by a fieldwalker in an English ploughed field.

Not to scale

Cross-and-pellet type reverses with sloping-line rims.

Obverses of sloping-line rimmed pieces with cross-and-pellet reverses.

Not to scale

Other possibly 15th century leaden pieces that seem strongly influenced by coin designs.

Not to scale

Other possibly 15th century leaden pieces that seem strongly influenced by coin designs.

Not to scale

More leaden pieces that probably date from the 15th century.

Decorative seals like these would have passed through the hands of numerous working men, women and children in the 15th century.

Not to scale

Chapter 6

Tudor Tokens & Tallies

The Tudor dynasty spanned 118 remarkable years that produced some of the most famous monarchs of English history and spawned adventurers such as Drake, Raleigh and Frobisher, and nurtured the literary genius of Shakespeare, Marlowe, and Spencer. It also witnessed London's emergence as the world's greatest city, the birth of consumerism, and the beginnings of empire. But from our petty viewpoint as token and tally enthusiasts let us not forget that one of those monarchs was Henry VIII, the king largely responsible for our present deficit of knowledge concerning medieval ecclesiastical practices. His destruction of monasteries cost us dearly in written records and left us to piece together the remnants in much the same way that archaeologists try to piece together fragments of medieval cathedral windows shattered by Henry VIII's vandals.

Fortunately his daughter, Elizabeth I, made some recompense when she bequeathed to us the remarkable document that follows. I've altered none of the delightful spellings because they catch the flavour of the age. A couple of sentences may sound familiar; they receive frequent quotation in the introductory paragraphs of books about 17th century copper tokens. But there's so much more for leaden token and tally collectors here, in addition to the queen's wonderful turns of phrase. Oh, brave *old* world that had such people in it!

Whereas in the beginninge of our reigne, to the greate honour and profytt of us and all our people, WE did restore and reduce the moneys of our realm from drosse and base matter unto fyne gould and fyne silver, which by God's favor we entend to contynue and maynteyn; yet because the rate and division of other money is such as at the present tyme requiereth, and cannot well be altered, as that with any convenyence any smaller money may be made thereof than a penny or threefarthinge; nevertheless we have been often informed, and doo perceyve what greate necessity our loving subjects have of smaller moneys, halfpence and farthings, and cheifly what loss and hinderaunce the poor sorte doo susteyne by the lacke thereof, whereof we have pytifull consideration, and bendynge ourselfe to the remedy of the same, diverse devices have been tendered to US and our previe councell, as well showing meanes howe the same small moneys might be made both fair in showe and suficyent in quantitie ; as alfo complaninge of a long contynued and yet a very intollerable and arrogant disorder used by private persons in makinge of tokens of leade and tynne, and generally coyned and put out instead of such small monys by grocers, vintners, chandlers and alehouse-keepers, and diverse other persons, therein manyfestly derogatinge from our princelye honour and royale dignytie, which complaint we have considered as very juste and resonable; but because the devyces offered therewith have all tended to the breach of the fyne standerd of our coyne in such fmall money and wanted a mixture for the fame of course and base alloye, to the slander and discredit of our fyne silver moneys, now being we have rejected all the same devices; and, yet waying with ourselves the greate disorder used in the sayde tokens, and howe that our said subjects have greate losse, and no manner of profytable ease thereby, whilst they serve not in anywise to be utterred or payde agayne but only at that shoppe or place where they were first receved. Therefore we doo, by these presents, freightly forbid and command that none of the sayde former tokens, or any such like of what device or invention soever from or after the Feast of All Saints next cominge, shall be made or used without our specyall warrent and comyssion in that behalfe, upon payne that the person or persons makinge or using the same shall suffer imprisonmente of their bodies by the space of one whole year; and that moreover paye such fyne to our use as shall be settled by our previe councell in the Star Chamber at Westminster. And forasmuch as upon great deliberacion we well perceyve that of necessitie our said subjects must either have halfpence and farthings, or else tokens to supplie the sted thereof; and because that such small moneys cannot be made of the fyne silver of our moneys whilst the same are

Some developments in English token shapes, sizes, designs during the 16th century.

Small lead tokens with a single letter on one or both faces may be Tudor agricultural tallies.

An attractive portcullis, mimicking a coin.

A pyramid of three initials on a lead token may have been a Tudor precursor of the copper tokens that appeared in the 17th century after the Civil War.

Henry VIII's base silver farthing was so small it slipped through calloused fingers and became lost far too easily.

Not to scale

They may look like very early medieval pieces; but these plain cross lead tokens, with or without pellets, may have imitated the base silver farthings briefly issued by Tudor monarchs.

Not to scale

at 5s the oz, but that they will be so small as that they can neither be well kept or used in payment. Wherefore, for the ease of our sayde subjects, and to serve their necessitie in this case, we have taken order that by our authoritie there shall be pledges or tokens made of pure and fyne copper of halfpence and farthings, whereof every pledge of the half-penny shall waie 24 gr and that of the farthing 12 gr.

Fine words, but they buttered no parsnips. The promised copper pledges never circulated, and the *poore sorte* had no ease from their want of small change. They had to make do with leaden tokens and tallies, and the Continental black money that continued to flow in because the bullion silver price was so high, until the Stuarts sat on England's throne. And here is another anomaly: The queen wrote of a *long contynued...greate losse...* [caused by] *...tokens of leade and tynn ... put out... by grocers, vintners, chandlers, ale-house-keepers, and diverse other persons.* But where are those tokens? The above document dates from the *late* 1500s. Elizabeth I had by then reigned almost 40 years; yet she issued no farthings and precious few halfpence.

Barely more than 40 years later in Stuart times, grocers, vintners, chandlers, alehouse-keepers and diverse other persons up and down the land began issuing their own *copper* farthing tokens. The pieces were neatly executed and lettered, bearing names, initials, (partial) addresses, puns, rebuses and eye-catching pictorial elements. Surely such sophistication did not spring up *sui generic* overnight?

Leaden precursors serving as change, and as sales-promoting message bearers, must have existed in large quantities during her reign to ruffle the great queen's feathers to such degree. Yet leaden finds from the Tudor years bearing pictorial designs and place-names remain scarce. Could it be that these types circulated only in cities, towns and larger villages, and that few were lost on fields now searched by detectorists? It is doubtful.

Numerous 17th century copper tokens intended to circulate in urban areas found their way onto ploughed fields, often via middens, and are recovered by detectorists. Losses of leaden pieces ought to have occurred in similar ways. Perhaps Elizabeth I was mistaken and the culprits were all London tavern-keepers? An extract from J.H. Burn's **Descriptive Catalogue Of London Traders, Tavern & Coffee House Tokens Current In The 17th Century** suggests otherwise:-

A book of accounts of Nicholas Ball, marketman, of Chudleigh, Devonshire, supplies some facts as to the cost of leaden tokens at that time. [ie during the reign of Elizabeth I]. The entries read -

Expences: [sic] *January 24th, 1562, Item: paid for an nyron with a prynt, and for lead, and for smiting of my tokens, 3 shilling*

February 23rd, 1566. Item: paid for 2 pounds of lead for tokens, and for making of the same to tokens, 22 pence.

This is Continental black money that circulated unofficially in Tudor England. Made from copper and perhaps one-farthing's worth of silver, it was acceptable as change to any poor customer seeking a halfpenny loaf with only a penny to spend.

These Tudor lead tokens would have proved just as acceptable at times when black money temporarily dried-up and monarchs failed to deliver on their promises to mint low denomination silver.

Another Continental interloper.

And its English leaden equivalent.

Not to scale

This is what a Tudor worker saw when he was fortunate enough to glimpse an Edward VI halfcrown.

It gave him the confidence to trust this leaden piece as change.

Not to scale

February 23rd, 1567. Item: paid for lead and for tokens for two years past, 26 pence.

Nicholas Ball's business must have expanded rapidly for him to need a continuous supply of lead tokens. Either that or they were lost at a steady rate in and around Chudleigh.

It deserves mention that the alehouse-keepers disparaged by Her Majesty earned their livings from much more than sales of alcohol. The alehouse probably served as a local shop and warehouse for all manner of goods delivered there because it offered a convenient collection and supply point. Alehouse lead tokens might therefore have strayed far from home to become losses.

One further piece of evidence about quantities before we look at some Tudor tokens and tallies that have come to light. In 1611 (just eight years after the death of Elizabeth I) statesman Sir Robert Cotton had the task of advising James I on how to increase the royal income. Cotton wrote:-

The benefit of the King will easily fall out, if he restrain retailers of victuals and small wares from using their own tokens [...] for in and about London there are above three thousand who cast yearly five pounds apiece of leaden tokens [...] and all the rest of this realme cannot be inferior to the city in proportion.

The cessation of most ecclesiastical tokens and tallies in 1535-40 would, no doubt, have included earlier types still used in connection with pilgrimages, charity and agricultural work; but the courtiers and others to whom Henry VIII sold Church lands would soon have needed their own tallies to control and pay labourers when the monks quit. Perhaps the 16th century proliferation of lead pieces bearing no religious references, but with single roman letters on one or both faces, had some connection with these events. Frequently discovered on arable land, often well away from settlements, they must surely have performed tallying functions in the increasingly productive Tudor agricultural cycle. Who can tell at this distance whether a piece with one letter on each face is recording a Christian and a family name, or one letter for a name and the other abbreviating the name of a parish, village or town?

Use of fixed surnames, begun by the Normans, had become widely established across England in the 16th century. There is even some leaden evidence to show that the well-known practice of using a pyramid of three letters (family name above, husband's and wife's first names below) very commonly seen on 17th century copper tokens, had begun in Tudor times.

Although ornate crosses appeared less frequently on Tudor tokens, many leaden pieces depicting a simple long-cross, and usually with one, two, three or four pellets in each segment, proliferated. Some with this design may date back to early long-cross pennies; but it's equally possible that those with a portcullis on the other face imitated the base silver farthings issued by Henry VIII and Edward VI. (Elizabeth issued a similar halfpenny in 1582.)

Tudor leaden tokens certainly copied the designs on other coins - and not always English issues. As we saw when discussing Boy Bishop tokens, which encompassed the Tudor years, reticence to duplicate full legends meant that borders were often filled with largely meaningless lettering; but we can still detect the influence of money on lead token mould makers.

The popularity of the Tudor Rose as an image on leaden tokens can be traced to the same image on coins of the realm.

Although the workers who used these crude pieces may never have handled a sovereign or ryal, the mould makers surely had ships depicted on gold coins in mind when they carved these vessels.

This is a very well-known image on 17th century copper tokens - a stick of candles being dipped in tallow - a symbol often used by chandlers. This leaden piece must have served the same purpose as change in a Tudor chandler's shop.

This piece appears to depict a Thames waterman rowing his craft. His purse must have contained many tokens and tallies similar to those we have discussed in this chapter.

Not to scale

Tudor double eagles were almost as popular as Tudor rampant lions.

The 18th century numismatist, P. Snelling, recorded these Elizabethan tokens as engravings in one of his books. The piece dated 1599 seems to be a butcher's token issued by R.C. and showing a cow about to be slaughtered. This would be a most interesting piece if it ever existed and was not a mere figment of Mr. Snelling's imagination.

Not long after looking at those engravings I received a rather poorly focused image of a lead token find depicting a cow in a very similar position, though facing right, not left.

Then another poorly focused image arrived. It shows the pictorial element on an item of French black money. It's a cow, and part of the circle dividing the animal and legends seems duplicated on the piece in Snelling's engraving above.

Not to scale

Chapter 7

Post-Tudor Developments

Ten years into his reign, James I's personal extravagances obliged him to take up Sir Robert Cotton's suggestion for a lucrative suppression of leaden tokens as a means of adding to the royal coffers. In 1613 he made a proclamation which began:-

In times past some toleration has existed in my realms of tokens of lead commonly known by the name of farthing tokens, that pass between vintners, tapsters, chandlers, bakers, and other like tradesmen and their customers; whereby such small portions and quantities of things vendible [...] might be conveniently bought and sold, without enforcement to buy more wares than would serve for use and occasion. But WE object that the manner of issuing [these lead tokens] and the use of them, as they pass only between customers, does not that public good which might, by a more general use, be effected. They are subject to counterfeiting, loss, and deceit; for sometimes they are refused as doubtful things, and sometimes, by the death or removal of those who gave them, are lost and discredited. And also, that it is some derogation to the royal prerogative that such tokens should be allowed to have currency, in any degree, with the lawful money of the realm. Therefore WE, being willing to continue to my subjects the good arising from the use of such small moneys ...[....]...have given power and authority, by letters patent, to John, Lord Harrington of Exeter [...] and his [...] assigns, to make such a competent quantity of farthing tokens of copper as might be conveniently issued amongst my subjects.

The king went on to declare that it was not his intention to give these copper tokens the status of money; nor to force his subjects to accept them in payments; but that the new tokens were to pass for the value of farthings within the king's realms *with the liking and consent of my loving subjects*. As for the old leaden tokens, they were prohibited from use *as from the Feast of St John the Baptist*.

Fine words, just as in Tudor days; but the greed of everyone involved in a scheme that sought to monopolise production of tokens extrinsically valued at one farthing but intrinsically worth rather less given the prevailing price of copper, doomed the project from the outset. The worst abuses with these copper tokens (variously known as Harrrington farthings, Lennox farthings, Richmond farthings and Maltravers farthings, depending on who paid the king most for the monopoly licence) probably occurred during the succeeding reign. But from the outset, and without the liking and consent of the poor, rich merchants and employers grabbed the opportunity to buy freshly minted tokens at (for example) 20 shillings sterling for 21 shillings in token face-value, then to stuff them into workers' outstretched hands at the rate of 48 for a shilling's worth of work.

By 1631 counterfeiters had leapt on the bandwagon, selling their lightweight copies at 20 shillings sterling for 26 shillings in copper tokens face-value. The final scenes were played out in 1644, two years after the flight of Charles I from London.

In his book, **Tradesmen's Tokens** (London, 1849) J.Y. Akerman provides a sorry description of ... *the doors of the Parliament House daily besieged by fruit-women, fish-women and others who obtain a livelihood by selling small wares. Some of these poor creatures had [...] as much as ten or twenty shillings in farthing tokens, while many tradesmen had even sixty pounds worth. It was supposed that at this time there was about £100,000 in farthings dispersed throughout the kingdom, their sole value being now the weight of copper only.*

That leaden token farthings continued to circulate throughout those uneasy decades is confirmed by several proclamations against them during both reigns. A few have come to light depicting crowns

These dated pieces range over 200 years and confirm the widespread use of lead throughout the 17th and 18th centuries.

Not to scale

Tokens circulated as small change and as tallies, tickets and receipts.

Not to scale

similar to the usual design on Harrington and Maltravers coppers. A few more have come to light carrying dates from the early 1600s right through to the late 1700s. (Bear in mind that it took until the 1770s and the reign of George III for the government to make any serious attempt to strike enough copper farthings to supply the entire country's needs, and until 1821 for the Royal Mint to achieve that goal with a minting of two and three-quarter million copper farthings.) But the most frequently encountered leaden pieces throughout the 17th and 18th centuries were undoubtedly those that carried little more than the initials of the issuer; some uniface, others with one or two initials on both faces, more with initials and simple ornamentation such as enigmatic petals. Clearly the issuer expected his/her initials to be recognised, perhaps as an assurance that the piece would be redeemed for an agreed value.

Putting myself in the situation of a poor customer buying bread, and given the choice of accepting a Harrington copper farthing on which only the king's name appeared, which might be a counterfeit, which I could not be certain another local shop would accept, and which even the baker might decline next time if he caught rumours of counterfeits in the neighbourhood ... or of taking a crudely made lead farthing that had the baker's initials clearly marked ... well, I'd back the baker against the king on any market-day.

Another huge group of leaden pieces had numerals with and without accompanying initials. These will be dealt with in the chapter that follows. We are left with a bewildering assortment of pieces carrying designs such as anchors, grids, arrows, cross-keys, which might be elements from more complex designs seen on the arms of tradesmen's guilds. (Bakers included anchors in their arms; watermen had grids; apothecaries had arrows; and fishmongers had cross-keys) But what explanations can we offer for animals, birds, human heads, bottles, wine glasses, boats, bells, and so many more? Some were probably counters for use in board games; others may have served as tickets and passes; a number could be merchant marks; the better made and more ornate may represent early advertising pieces. All that we can say with certainty is that further research may enlighten us.

The lettered types depicted include single, double, treble letters. There are also examples of retrograde letters; the mould maker may have erred ... or did he/she deliberately make the lettering this way to catch the eye? Look also at the ligatured letters in which two letters share one leg. The many lettering styles reflect two centuries during which such pieces changed hands.

Not to scale

Not to scale

Not to scale

Not to scale

Not to scale

Not to scale

Some of these may have been children's toys. Other, more sophisticated pieces might have been used as passes and tickets for beaters on country estates.

Not to scale

We can only guess that these were merchant marks. Local research - on gravestones for example - can sometimes reveal a merchant mark that also occurs on a token.

The importance of rivers and coastal waters as transport and commercial routes is hinted at by finds of tokens and tallies depicting vessels of many types and sizes.

Not to scale

Were these simply bakers' farthing tokens, or were they tallies for cargo handlers?

Not to scale

Queen Elizabeth and King James prohibited tavern pieces.
(Note: The piece depicting a human head is from a London tavern - The Looking Glass.)

Were these given to bell ringers ... or were they used as games counters at the Bell Tavern ?

Not to scale

The symbolism within the designs on many of these pieces is lost to our modern minds; but who would deny their fascination?

Not to scale

Not to scale

Grid patters can be seen on the arms of the Watermen's Guild. On the other hand, could these be agricultural tallies given to farm labourers for ploughing and/or harrowing work?

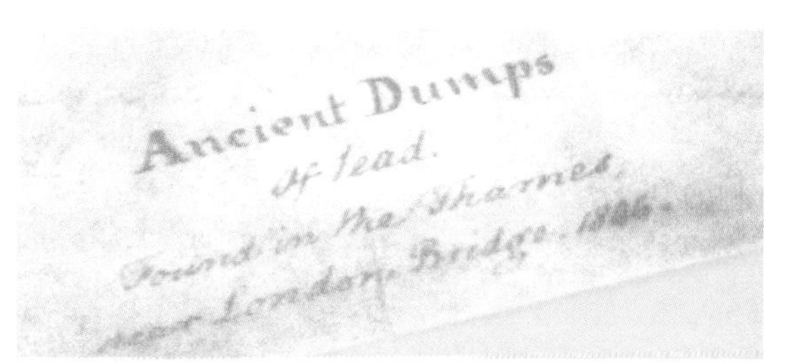

I spotted this faded label at the Cuming Museum in London. It records the use of the word dump as the name once given to crude leaden pieces.

Not to scale

Chapter 8

Post-Tudor Agricultural Tallies

Agricultural Enclosure gathered momentum in England around 1500 and had largely run its course by 1830. In parishes across the land ancient open fields, unfenced meadows and rough pastures disappeared, leaving perhaps one-third of parishioners as independent yeomen who owned their own acres, or tenant farmers now renting fields from the lord of the manor, who remained the major landlord; and two-thirds of parishioners as landless and/or unemployed.

One, perhaps foreseeable, development witnessed a huge rise in crime in late Elizabethan times; but a glance at the statistics reveals that the commonest crime amounted to no more than being *a sturdy beggar* - one fit for work who fails to find work and so begs in the street for food. Elizabeth ordered that all sturdy beggars must be whipped and sent back to the parish they had newly arrived from; but the problem of beggars was not adequately dealt with until the establishment of union workhouses in the 19th century.

Meanwhile, inflation and poor harvests took their toll on small farmers. Many tenants, unable to find the rent, had, even by 1600, given up and joined the labourers or the paupers; some small owners had sold out to larger neighbours, gambling all on getting and keeping a labourer's job, or of making a successful relocation from country to town.

Parish social structure now had five strata: landed gentry; fairly prosperous independent middle-sized yeoman farmers; a few tenant farmers clinging on and praying for two or three good harvests in a row; a waged workforce who sold their labour where they could and scratched a little extra food from a patch of garden or an allotment; and an underclass of paupers totally dependent on charity. How might such social and economic structures have effected the use (and loss) of leaden tallies on enclosure land?

Let's imagine a Kentish yeoman farmer named Edward Fletcher working his fields in the mid-17th century. Despite his large family, Edward knows he will needs additional labour at certain times of year for sowing, harvesting, perhaps when lambing and shearing. He also knows the folly of paying wages in cash to casual men who might spend it at the village inn before sowing, harvesting, lambing or shearing are completed. Instead he uses lead tallies, probably cast in a mould he keeps for that very purpose and bearing the letter F because other farmers in the neighbourhood usually address him as Fletcher, or Goodman Fletcher.

Crucially each tally also has a value marked; a figure representing hours worked, or sacks filled, or sheep shorn, or other work counted. If he happens to have a brother who farms on neighbouring land, Edward will probably have two letters - EF - on his tallies to ensure that he does not end up footing someone else's wage bill.

Finds of crudely fashioned and dumpy lead pieces bearing letter-and-number combinations have frequently turned up on English arable fields. Their thickness and size suggest post-Tudor origins, but very few have exhibited the triangular three-letter style so often seen on 17th century lead and copper farthing tokens.

It seems that despite years of toil alongside her husband, Mrs Goodwife Fletcher's Christian name initial would not often have featured on the farm's tallies. This observation seems to hold true throughout England; a 17th century lead find bearing one or two initials and numbers that are not a date is highly

Shown here are examples of early single, double and triple letter tallies.
The crudely executed numerals and lettering on other pieces also suggest early manufacture.
Note the three pieces with ornate rims which might have come from gentry farms.

Not to scale

Not to scale

likely to be a tally. Supporting evidence might come from finds bearing the same initials but different numbers. Thus EF 1 tallies might well turn up on fields where EF 2 tallies are found. They represent different amounts of work tallied.

Neater and better-made pieces bearing one or two initials, with and without numerals, might have emanated from a gentleman farmer's property. The gentry often retained some of their labourers, tying them to a cottage and demanding any and every sort of work for a pittance paid twice yearly. Such economic relationships required no tallying.

Nevertheless, at sowing, harvesting and other times extra hands might have been taken on and subjected to a tallying system. This could account for the few ornate 17th century tallies that turn up. A gentleman farmer is more likely to have asked his gunsmith to engrave a die for striking tallies rather casting them in a crude mould, perhaps embellishing the design with a family crest, or at least an ornate border. Non-estate labourers coming onto the grounds as beaters might have required numbered gate passes that modern finders mistake for tallies.

If we move forward and look at tally finds reasonably dated to the 18th and early 19th century we discover many more two and three-letter pieces; we also encounter pieces bearing a wider range of numerals. Rising populations meant that identity had to be more specifically stated to avoid confusion. Several farmers with a surname beginning with F might by that date have lived in the same district. So Edward Fletcher's heir, Edward James Fletcher, might have used EJF, though more likely to appear in a straight line and not in pyramid style. Occasionally two men from different families shared a business, especially one growing horticultural crops. Their tokens might feature four letters.

Some farmers had begun to spell out their names fully, even occasionally including the name of their village. More complex numbering reflected greater diversity in cropping, and a wider range of weights and measures used on many farms. Adding further complexity, self-employed tradesmen such as blacksmiths, cordwainers (shoemakers), fellmongers, carters, wheelwrights, fullers (who treated cloth), maltsters and more moved into prosperous districts and set up businesses of their own, some using tallies or lead tickets now indistinguishable from agricultural tallies.

In 1601 a new Poor Law Act came into force, requiring each parish to care for its own destitute with money raised by rates. In some areas the homeless were directed to workhouses where, in exchange for food and shelter, they toiled without wages at a variety of tasks, some out-of-doors. Such regimentation and bureaucracy encouraged the use of tallies, partly because many workhouse overseers were also local yeomen farmers performing parochial duties voluntarily and well accustomed to this method of control. Lost tallies from these institutions have turned up on fields close to former workhouses.

One series within agricultural tallies has generated widespread interest in collecting leaden pieces, partly because the colourful social histories of workers who handled them have been vividly recounted in recent years. Despite their name, these pieces are most certainly agricultural tallies, though *hop tokens* is too familiar to alter now for the sake of paranumismatic accuracy.

The fact that Enclosure began early in south-east England and that many yeoman farmers in the region already improved the fertility of their fields by manuring and crop rotation gave Kent a head start when hop growing commenced in the early 1500s. Flemish weavers and Dutch pilgrims visiting Canterbury preferred their native hop-flavoured beer to English ale and may have passed on the secrets of successful hop growing to farmers in the area. Good supplies of local timber for hop poles and charcoal for drying provided added impetus for concentration of production in East Kent, though hops were grown in more than a dozen English counties by 1650.

A massive boost came in the 1720s when a new brew called "porter" became the preferred tipple of porters working in London's docks. Its bitterness derives from generous use of hops, so as porter drinking spread throughout the country demand for Kentish hops increased accordingly. By the 1800s more than 70,000 acres of hops grew every year in the county, far more than local farm labourers could pick. References to *strangers who came for the hopping* occur in many parish records in the 1650s, though the peak in these invasions occurred post-1850s when more than 80,000 flooded into East Kent every autumn.

The pickers, often entire families of poor Londoners who came yearly to the same farm, lived in makeshift encampments in the hop gardens. They picked in gangs, filling one-gallon buckets and sacks (pokes) with hop cones, then topping-up larger containers that held a bushel (8 gallons). The amount paid per bushel depended on the quality of the hops when inspected by a hop factor who visited each farm as picking drew to a close. Meanwhile the pickers received *tokens* as records of work done.

Widely used numbering systems included 1, 6, 12, 30, 60 and 120-bushel pieces, and a more complicated 1, 2, 3, 4, 5, 6, 7, 8, 10, 11, 12, 15, 20, 25, 30, 50, 60 and 120 set that could have served to record the one to eight gallons in a bushel (with 9 omitted to avoid confusion with 6), or quantities of bushels up to 120, which was probably a cartload.

Although the hop tokens depicted in this group have clearly evolved from the crudity of earlier times, they retain a rustic, locally-made appearance that suggests a self-sufficient farmer producing his own moulded tallies, or possibly persuading the local blacksmith to turn out a batch as and when needed.

Not to scale

Not to scale

Throughout the 17th century pickers averaged one-penny per bushel for their labours, rising to three-halfpence by the early 19th century.

The earliest hop tokens were probably locally made and crudely cast lead pieces similar to the tallies used for other crop picking by farmers throughout England, but at the peak of prosperity in Victorian times several growers took great pride in the appearance of their tallies. Some were struck rather than cast, and several bore ornate images of hops, oast houses, hop pokes, or even local wildlife.

Another group of leaden pieces that merit inclusion in this chapter might have served as tallies associated with milling. Many have come to light not too distant from the sites of watermills and windmills. They have no numerals moulded on their surfaces, but they depict what look very much like grinding wheels or, in some cases, like windmill sails. Three have come to my attention that certainly depict complete windmills. One of those three is known only from a rubbing of its design and lettering that names the mill and gives the initials of the miller, as well as a year of manufacture. Were these pieces used as tallies or receipts for sacks of corn brought for grindings that had to await favourable winds? I want to alert readers to watch out for such pieces when searching around the sites of once busy mills.

As hop growing and the work force expanded the pieces used on many farms took on a unity of form and lettering that strongly suggests a few makers cornered the market. They supplied utilitarian tallies with lettering and numerals struck in bold relief. Made from a harder alloy than in earlier periods, they could withstand rough handling and were unlikely to be mistaken for incorrect values.

Not to scale

The vast majority of leaden agricultural tallies were disc-shaped, but oddities were made, perhaps as aids to identification.

To earn one of these coveted 120-bushel hop tokens pickers had to fill 960 one-gallon buckets with hop cones no bigger than a finger-end.

Not to scale

The prosperity and pride of mid-19th century hop growers reflects in these ornate pieces. Queen Victoria's bust on the Bosworth farm piece suggests that some farmers in non-hop growing districts also took pride in their tallies.

Not to scale

Watermills and windmills like these once dotted the English countryside. Farmers who carted corn for grinding may have received tallies for sacks left at the mill to await a favourable wind or river flow. Two lead tokens depicting windmills are shown - one dated 1708. The pencil rubbing is from a lead piece that shows a windmill and gives the miller's initials and a date.

This Victorian brass token clearly demonstrates the use of such pieces as receipts or deposits for sacks. Earlier leaden pieces probably served similar purposes.

Not to scale

These pieces clearly depict windmill sails. Compare them with the drawing of an early windmill's sails on the previous page.

These pieces clearly depict waterwheels, each displaying a central hub or axle, as seen in the medieval drawing on the previous page.

These pieces show what look very much like waterwheels.

These pieces look like grinding stones.

Not to scale

Chapter 9

Communion Tokens

Scottish communion tokens were probably first made in the 1560s, but the most ancient pieces that can be dated with certainty from ecclesiastical records belong to the early 1600s. Although made from lead, they have little in common with any English products so far as usage goes, apart from communion tokens from south of the border mentioned below.

Nevertheless, some might easily be mistaken for English agricultural tallies of similar age because, as we have seen in previous chapters, the designs upon many mid-17th century English tallies were quite stark - often no more than two or three letters and a number that could be a date. Such a description comfortably fits many early Scottish communion tokens if we know nothing about the meaning of those embossed initials and numerals, so let's find out a little more concerning the history of these often puzzling pieces.

As with so much church history, we must go back to Continental practices to dig up Scottish roots. They show that in the mid-1500s, at a time when the Holy Catholic Church and the Reformed Church of Martin Luther's making were struggling for supremacy, authorities on both sides feared breakaway movements within their own ranks as much as they feared each other. It was therefore decided (who first nobody knows) that the faithful must carry some mark of their worthiness to participate in Holy Communion services. All involved would have been comfortably familiar with the use of leaden tokens and tallies in many other facets of daily life, so lead tokens of identity would have seemed perfectly natural.

In Scotland the time of greatest danger to Reformed Church supporters occurred during the reign of Catholic Stuarts who persecuted Protestants and diligently burned them alive whenever they caught them at their heretical services. By issuing leaden tokens to the faithful, the elders could exclude spies. But the tokens were not simply handed out to anyone who claimed to be a church member. Rigorous questioning and testing of religious knowledge first took place, and questions were also asked and answered concerning each person's good character. Such strict discipline was essential when large outdoor gatherings of the faithful took place (the Stuarts had closed their churches) in what everyone prayed would remain secret places.

Another reason for holding three or four large services rather than many smaller ones arose from a shortage of church plate. Sacred vessels were confiscated and melted down whenever Catholics attacked and desecrated a Protestant church. Thus it became necessary for small congregations to share whatever silver plate they had managed to save from destruction.

Ritual and ceremony soon developed around the moulding and casting of tokens. Only trusted blacksmiths were allowed to melt down old pieces and to recast the new ones required for a future gathering. Large open-air services that occurred a few times each year often required the manufacture of hundreds, occasionally thousands, of tokens, and ministers had to be on hand at the casting operations to take up the new pieces, to break the moulds at the end of the process, and to keep the tokens safe until the time came to issue them to selected communicants.

We know from chance finds that some tokens must have become accidentally lost, and that all in a particular batch were hardly ever completely recycled by melting. Enough have survived to make Scottish communion token collecting a viable branch of paranumismatics. Indeed, it has become a worldwide

A fine collection of early lead Scottish communion tokens.

Not to scale

A fine collection of early lead Scottish communion tokens.

Not to scale

interest because so many Scots driven from their mother country by persecutions and poverty took the practice of making and distributing leaden tokens to wherever they settled. A few even took old communion tokens that had escaped earlier melting down processes, intending to have the relics placed in their coffins.

Ministers who quitted Scotland at such times would have taken un-melted tokens in their possession out of the country rather than allow them to fall into Catholic hands. That's probably how the practice spread south of the border. It is also known that splinter groups from the Scottish Secession churches took root in northern England and used names such as the Free Church, the Scotch Church and the Relief Church. Most of those small groups began to make and distribute lead communion tokens to the faithful in England. They eventually amalgamated in the 1870s as The Presbyterian Church of England. By that time persecutions had long ago ceased. Stock tokens could be purchased openly from ecclesiastical suppliers - pictorial specimens in copper and brass embellished with biblical texts. They look attractive, but they lack the appeal of the early crudely fashioned lead.

A brief description of an outdoor communion service helps to explain some of the lettering and numbers found on early pieces, which were in fact tickets or passes rather than tokens. Having successfully passed the minister's tests regarding knowledge of the Lord's Prayer, the Creed, and the Ten Commandments, and the elders' probings for any hint of scandal in his/her life, the successful applicant would have been handed a token and sworn to secrecy about the appointed venue for the next service.

The chosen place was often a clearing in a wooded glen where dozens of tables and chairs were set out, with a minister seated at the head of each. The participant's ticket sometimes had a number preceded by the letter "T" indicating at which table he should sit. Some pieces omit this letter, the participant having been informed by word beforehand about where to sit. Other lettering on the token might have included two or three together with the first a letter "M". In that case the next letter or letters gave the minister's initials. (A group of three was often triangulated, as seen on English 17th century tokens).

One face of the token probably had the year of casting, often with another group of letters beginning with a "K". This indicated the kirk (church) or parish were the token was issued. Apart from occasional flourishes such as a border or (rarely) the depiction of a communion wine glass or decanter, very little else appears on these early pieces, which is why they are often not initially recognized as communion tokens when found.

So far as leaden tokens and tallies go, Scotland is poorly served apart from communion tokens. That's due in part to an abundance of small change throughout Scottish history; also to the fact that the common practice of making lead farthings to use as change fully satisfied needs at other times in many Scottish towns and villages. These lead farthing tokens are usually very plain affairs with no more than the shopkeeper's initials and the name of the town. Some have been mistaken for communion tokens.

Another very small group of Scottish pieces deserves mention. It seems that some old and unwanted lead communion tokens were re-used in the 19th century as *beggars' badges*, official licences given to selected paupers to beg in the streets. That may account for occasional finds of lead communion tokens with holes bored in them to take string.

Not to scale

Not to scale

19th century communion tokens were often made up from stock shapes and designs.

Not to scale

Obverse and reverse of a Scottish communion token found in northern England.

Reverse of a leaden piece that may once have been a communion token; holed and stamped BB, perhaps for Beggar's Badge.

This is a genuine Scottish beggar's badge.

Obverses and reverses of two typical 19th century Scottish grocers' lead farthing tokens.

Not to scale

Chapter 10

Shycocks

More by coincidence than design, the turn of a page has taken us from some of the plainest pieces to types that *must* have striking embellishments to qualify for inclusion in this chapter. Without exception they display, usually on one face, an avian image - anything feathered, from a strutting pelican to a cocky sparrow. The list includes swans, peacocks, eagles, pigeons, parrots, pullets, long-eared owls, blackbirds, partridges and many that defy ornithological categorisation.

As finds they turn up throughout England, predictably more prolifically from counties with lots of arable land, and unexpectedly often very close to farm buildings rather than scattered across fields as other tallies and tokens usually come to light. A further and very puzzling likelihood is that finders will also report larger fragments of lead, some exhibiting featherlike markings, discovered not far from where the bird token losses occur.

About a year ago I stumbled on an account of a late-Victorian country childhood in which the writer recalled that he had earned 2d a day as a pigeon hunter in a newly sown field. He told of his prowess with a catapult, and put his success down to having a plentiful supply of lead ball ammunition dug up behind an ancient rifle range on a nearby army encampment.

I pounced on this information and decided that most tokens carrying images of birds had been cast in clay moulds by small boys who needed ammunition for their catapults. The birds they scribed in the mould were ritualistic images of birds they hoped to shoot down; the pieces were disc-shaped because a disc is easier to cast than a lead sphere; and the associated larger pieces of lead were the remnants of stockpiles made around places where young boys stoked fires to melt and cast their metal.

I felt quite satisfied with my deductions until a correspondent in **Treasure Hunting** magazine reported a most unusual find from Kent: among many fragments of lead she had turned up a complete leaden bird. The decoration on its body and wings closely matched similar decoration on the bases of seven more incomplete lead birds found nearby. Furthermore, she had a word to describe her find: it was a *shy cock*. The term meant little to me, but as so often happens, another correspondent from Cambridgeshire informed me not long afterwards that he had found parts of what looked like a nearly complete lead pheasant. He too said it was a shy cock. The phrase came before my eyes for a third time while I leafed through some dusty offerings in a second-hand bookshop a few days later and chanced upon William Hone's **Everyday Book**, first published in London in 1826. It gave the following account of boys at play in Georgian England:-

Shying at Leaden Cocks.
Probably in imitation of the barbarous custom of shying or throwing at the living animal, the cock was a representation of a bird, a beast, a man, a horse, or some device, with a stand projecting on all sides, but principally behind the figure. These were made of lead cast in moulds. They were shyed at with dumps from a small distance agreed upon by the parties, generally regulated by the size or weight of the dump, and the value of the cock. If the thrower overset or knocked down the cock, he won it; if he failed, he lost his dump.

As mentioned in a previous chapter, the word "dump" is recorded in the Cuming Museum, London as the term once used for crudely cast lead tokens. I read on:-

A cock was not allowed to have its stand extended behind more than its height and half; nor much thicker than the cock [...] But fraudulent cocks were made [...] with a

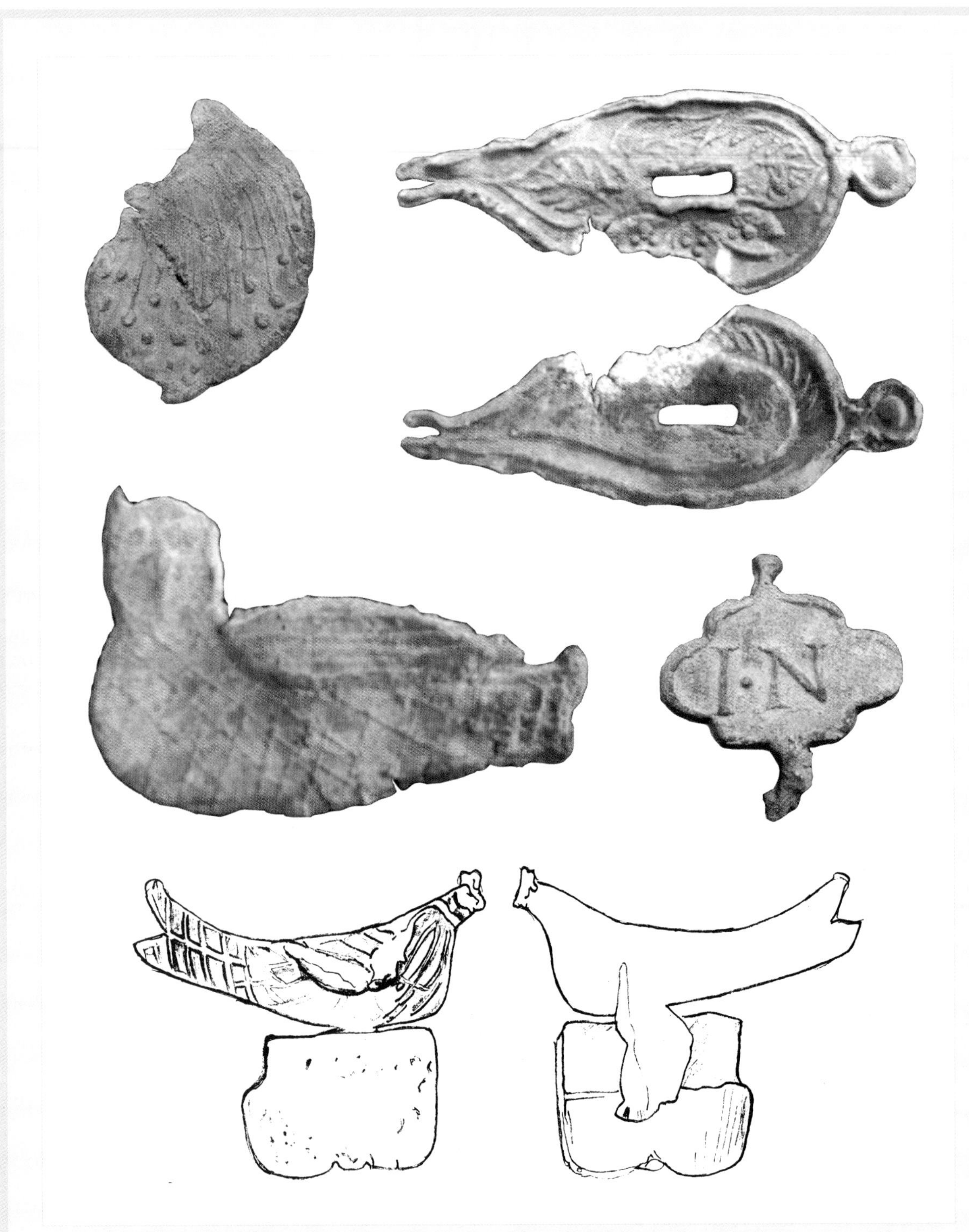

These were the targets in shy cocks games. The condition of many bear witness to the accuracy of boys when it comes to hurling missiles. But note the fine detail on wings ... and the initials on one of the bases. That must have been a home-made piece and not one sold in the shambles.

Not to scale

Not to scale

long stand behind and the body of the cock made thinner, by which means the cock bent upon being struck, and it was impossible to knock over.

There was more further down the page on how the game was played, and details of a source of ready-made cocks and dumps:-

The game was played at by two boys, each having a cock placed at a certain distance, generally about four or five feet asunder, the players standing behind their cocks, and throwing alternately. The cock was won by him who knocked it down. Cocks and dumps were exposed for sale on the butchers' shambles on a small board, and were the perquisite of the apprentices, who made them. [...] Many a pewter plate, and many an ale-house pot, were melted at this season for shying at cocks, which was as soon as fires were lighted in the autumn.

Another correspondent in Hone's book had this to say on the ancestry of the shy cocks game:

Throwing At Cocks
This brutal practice on Shrove Tuesday is still conspicuous in several parts of the kingdom...[...] In some places it was a common practice [in the last century] to put a cock into an earthen vessel made for the purpose, and to place him in such a position that his head and tail might be exposed to view. The vessel, with the bird in it, was then suspended across the street, about 12 or 13 feet from the ground, to be thrown at by such as chose to make trial of their skill. Twopence was paid for four throws, and he who broke the pot, and delivered the cock from his confinement, had him for a reward.

So I think we can now safely assign most dumpy lead pieces bearing images of birds to the category of gaming pieces, though in this case not a board game. It might also be reasonable to say that any piece with a neatly executed design and without initials on its other face could have been made by one of those poulterer's apprentices who was likely to have left one face blank so that a young player could scribe his initials (or mark) into the lead piece before play commenced. But any enterprising lad making his own ammunition for the game would surely have cut his initials into the mould before pouring molten lead. Ah, the delights of boyhood! Those initials offer scope for diligent researchers. Parish records might throw up the names of those who threw the missiles.

Bird images in a remarkable range of styles appear on these pieces, some displaying the naivety of children's work; other depicting birds in fine artistic detail.

Not to scale

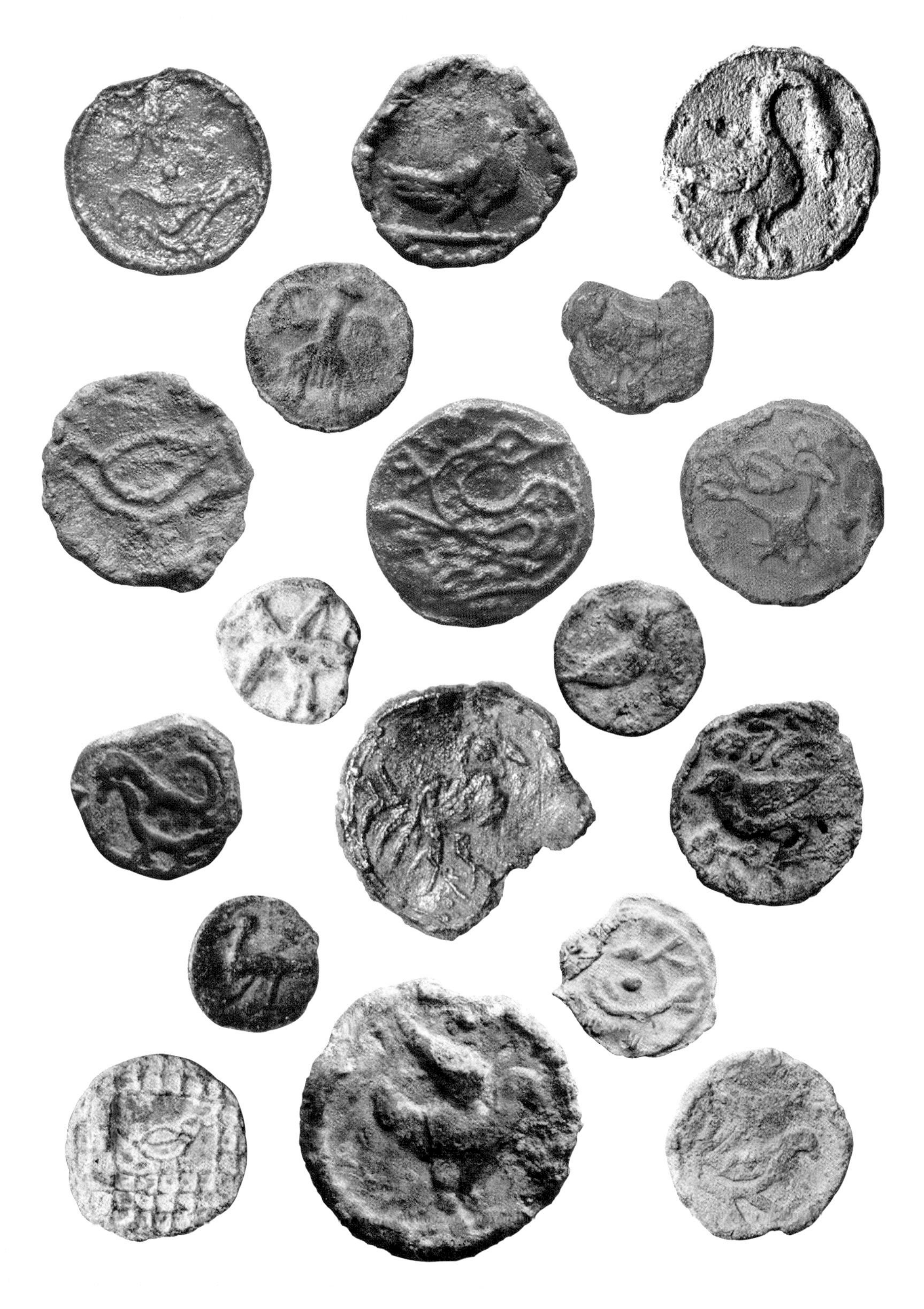

Not to scale

Chapter 11

Moulds

Moulded? Cast? Stamped? Struck?
How Were Leaden Tokens & Tallies Made?

Some confusion seems to arise when finders, collectors, dealers, museum curators, archaeologists and others who have to say or write anything about tokens and tallies broach the subject of manufacture. In most cases the problem does not arise from lack of understanding of the processes; rather from different interpretations of the four words heading this chapter. Let's see if author and readers of this book can agree on what they mean.

The discovery of several moulds for tokens and tallies has confirmed that open (one-piece) and bivalve (two-piece) moulds made from limestone, chalk, unfired clay, even a piece of broken pottery, were used to produce many pieces. A 1940s issue of *Sussex Life Magazine* carried an article on hop tokens in which the writer stated that some were made in wooden, plaster and brass moulds.

Examination of moulds that have so far come to light shows that, in addition to simple moulds for making one token or tally, many were cut/engraved/carved (those terms interchangeable) to achieve production of several tokens from a single pouring of molten lead. From two up to ten engravings connected by channels to allow the hot metal to flow through the mould were usually carved, and the two sides of the mould aligned with the aid of marks scored on their outsides, and/or by means of holes that passed through both parts.

Moulds for making uniface tokens also required two-piece moulds if the blank face of the token was to have a flat finish. A one-piece open mould produced a token with an obvious depression in the centre of the blank face caused by rapid shrinkage of the exposed molten lead.

Pouring of the molten lead - termed *moulding* or *casting* - inevitably left considerable amounts of waste metal (sprue) clinging to the newly cast tokens on removal from the mould. Much of the waste was cut or scraped off to go back into the melting pot, but tiny fragments remained around the edges of many pieces at the mould parting line. Some pieces also had small *tangs* or *tags* where the waste metal from a connecting channel was removed. These imperfections confirm that such a find is a cast or moulded token or tally.

What a pity that so little information has come down to us about other methods of producing leaden tokens and tallies. If we could see an example of the *nyron with a print* used by Nicholas Ball, the 16th century marketman mentioned in Chapter 6 to smite his own lead tokens we might experience great enlightenment. Or if we could closely examine one of the leaden pieces produced between 1569 and 1682 for the churchwardens of St Thomas' Church, Salisbury who paid various [black]smiths and bell-founders *for gravinge the stampe and strikinge* the tokens we'd be much wiser. (Reported in the *Numismatic Circular*, 1977) Certain it is that the stone, plaster, chalk and clay moulds mentioned above would not have survived a single blacksmith's blow. To resolve this problem I looked at an article about blacksmithing on the website of www.1911encyclopedia.org which had this to say:-

FORGING, the craft of the smith, or blacksmith differs from founding in that the metal is never melted...[but]...worked when it is in a plastic and more or less pasty condition. Consequently the tools used are in the main counterparts of the shapes desired, and they mould by impact; [but] the parallel between coining dies and forging dies does not go far. The blank for a coin is prepared to such exact dimensions that no surplus material is left over by the striking of the coin, which is struck while cold. But the blank used in die forging is generally a shapeless piece, taken without any preliminary preparation, a mere lump.

Part of a mould for casting the ubiquitous petal tokens. The small circular indents on the edges of the design were probably used as aids when turning a compass to scribe the petal outlines. [Photo courtesy: Salisbury Museum].

Part of a mould for casting another common design. The channels for entry and exit of the molten lead can be clearly seen. [Photo courtesy: Salisbury Museum].

This fragment of waste lead appears to have a trial casting from an unfinished mould for a cross-and-pellet type token.

Not to scale

This wonderful artefact is the obverse mould for making five pictorial medieval tokens. Enlargement of the photograph reveals that the stone slab had been ground flat to partially erase the designs of an earlier engraving. Glimpses of the erased work can be seen at top right, above the large location hole for matching the upper and lower parts. Photo: courtesy of Gloucester City Museum & Art Gallery.

Here is the reverse confirming that, in this case, uniface tokens were made, though any other same-sized slab could have produced a pictorial reverse. Photo: courtesy of Gloucester City Museum & Art Gallery.

Not to scale

At the verge of the heat to which it is raised, and under the intensity of the impact of hammer blows rained rapidly on the upper die, the metal yields, flows and fills the dies. A large amount of metal is squeezed out beyond the concavity of the forging dies, and this would, if allowed to flow over between the joints, prevent the dies from being closed on the forging, [so] this flash, as it is termed, must be removed.

We can now appreciate why the churchwardens paid to have their tokens made. And we can also appreciate that if semi-molten lead was forced by hammer blows into the mould the lettering and other details on the finished tokens and tallies would have been sharply outlined, as seen on many later hop tokens, for example. But I'm left wondering whether marketman Ball would have achieved results to match the blacksmiths' professional work.

Another method of making lead tokens must have been on Elizabeth I's mind when (see Chapter 6) she complained...

of a long contynued and yet a very intollerable and arrogant disorder used by private persons in makinge of tokens of leade and tynne, and generally coyned and put out instead of such smalI monys by grocers, vintners, chandlers and alehouse-keepers, and diverse other persons...

Coyned gives the clue. Many grocers, vintners, chandlers and alehouse-keepers who outlived Elizabeth by about 40 years - or their heirs more likely - made their own copper halfpenny tokens. I see no reason why lead blanks could not have been used in the same way as the copper blanks mentioned in what follows:-

The discovery of a coining press used to make 17th century copper tokens was reported in an 18th century issue of the *Gentleman's Magazine*. The press turned up in a house that had been occupied by Chesterfield apothecary, Edward Wood, who coined and issued his own copper token halfpennies a hundred years earlier. The description ran:

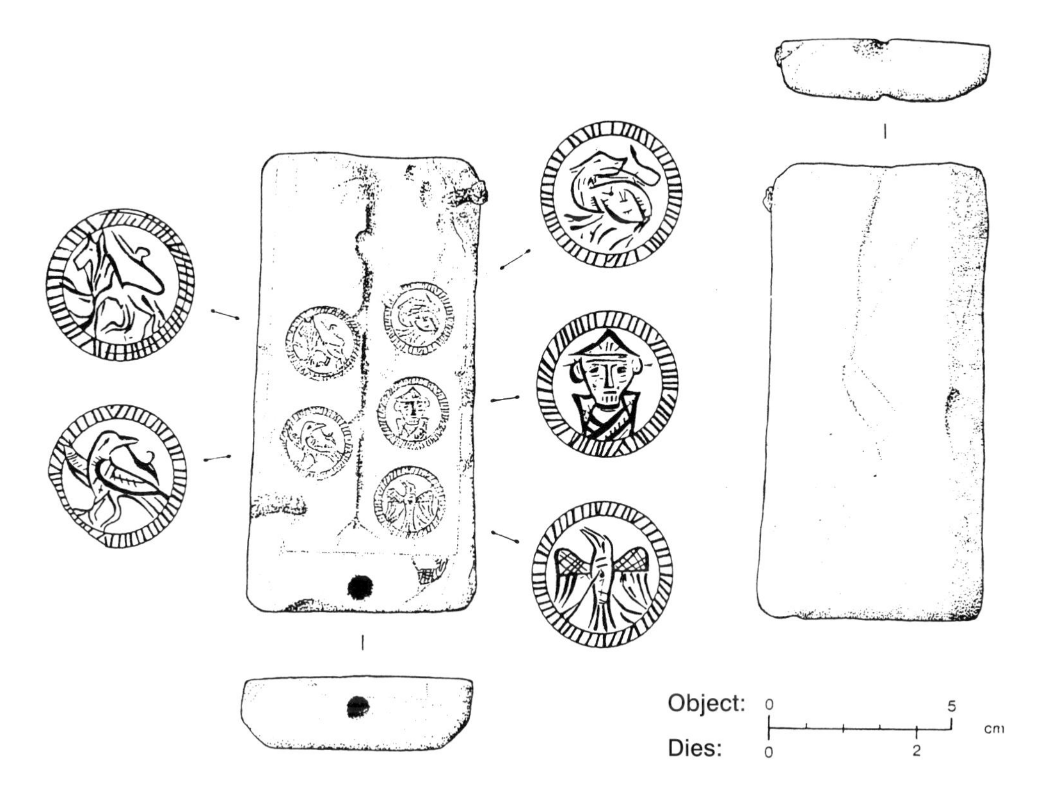

This line drawing shows the mould's shape, dimensions and token designs very clearly. Both parts of the mould were found during an excavation in Southgate Street, Gloucester. Photo: courtesy of Gloucester City Museum & Art Gallery.

The press consisted of four pieces of good oak, not less than four inches thick, and very strongly dove-tailed together. In the upper cross-piece was fastened an iron box with a female screw, through which there passed a stout iron screw of an inch or more diameter, to the bottom of which was fixed one of the dies; whilst the other was received into a square hole made in the bottom crosspiece, where it lay very steady as in a proper bed. The screw was wrought by hand, in the manner of a capstan, by means of four handles affixed to the top of it, of about nine inches long each. And thus, after the copper was reduced to a proper thickness, shorn to a size, and commodiously rounded, many hundreds of halfpence might be coined, by two persons, in a very short time, by a man we will suppose to ply the screw, and a woman or a boy to put on and take off the pieces. And yet I assure you, sir, these Chesterfield halfpennies were extremely well struck.

The **Newgate Callendar** is full of entries like the following from the days of hammered silver money:-

Joseph Peny was likewise Tried for High Treason, in Counterfeiting and making 20 Shillings of False and Unlawful Metal, to the likeness and similitude of the proper Coin of this Kingdom, which he did on the 28th of August. The Prisoner's Garret being search'd in Grays-Inn Lane, he was found sitting in a Chair, rubbing an Halfcrown between his Fingers, with a certain Powder the Clippers have to make it smooth. There were several other Halfcrowns that lay by him ready done, which were produced in Court; besides a Coining Press, Stamps, Screws, Molds and Flasks, with melting Pots, Scissers, and all Instruments fit for Coining, as also several Halfcrowns that were made of False Metal. The Prisoner alleg'd in his defence, that the things did not belong to him, nor the Room, but to one William Peny his Brother's Son, who was gone away. He, having nothing else to say, was found guilty of both Clipping and Coining. Verdict: Hanged.

In almost every case the *False Metal* referred to was a lead alloy. I'm sure that many of our well-made tokens must have been stamped or struck using such coining presses.

Chapter 12

A Brief Look At Cloth & Bag Seals

Lead's malleability made it ideally suited to the production of secure closures that could be crimped onto or around packages and containers, and then impressed with names or signs of ownership. We know the Romans did it because their two-part lead seals have turned up on numerous sites. And you may recall that in Chapter 2, I mentioned Blanchet's statement (op.cit.) that in 12th century France *lead seals were applied to cloth to indicate its source.*

So it seems that the practice never died out, and probably migrated to England long before Plantagenet monarchs decided to use complex seals on bales of cloth as a source of tax revenue. The short transitional step from seals to tokens and tallies must have been made all the shorter by the proliferation of cloth seals in every important marketplace. But the seals I want to mention briefly at the outset are the simpler types that go back to ancient usage.

Imagine two blank lead discs umbilically joined by a thin strip of lead that was bent to a U-shape and presented to the edge of a piece of cloth before the two discs were squeezed or hammered together to grip the material. During the squeezing or hammering impressions including pictorial designs, letters and numbers were embossed on the blank discs. Later, when the bale was opened and the lead seal broken it might have been thrown away with the two parts barely holding together.

Over time the strip connecting the two discs would probably break off, leaving what would look like two uniface lead tokens to await discovery centuries later. We have already seen when looking at token moulds that misalignment of the upper and lower parts must have happened now and again, resulting in what can seem like two thin uniface tokens corroded together...*or*...like a two-part seal as I have just described. Confusion seems even more likely if remnants of sprue remain on the edge of the piece; the remains of the connecting strip on a seal can look very similar.

Perhaps the best way forward when trying to differentiate between damaged seals and tokens is to keep in mind that cloth seals - by far the most commonly found - were official receipts for duty paid. They are highly likely to carry emblems of officialdom - crowns, lions, shields, eagles, portcullises, and similar marks of authority, especially if you find an early medieval specimen. It was in the reign of Edward I that officials known as "alnagers" were appointed to enforce the Assize of Measures which decreed that each piece of English cloth must be measured and subjected to a duty determined by its size, then marked with a leaden seal to confirm the duty as paid. Alnagers got their strange name thus:-

The Latin word for arm was *ulna* ... which became *aulne* in Old French and changed its meaning to *measure by the arm's length.* Old English altered that word to *ellne* then to *allne,* the *ell* part becoming a unit of measure equal to 45 breadths of a man's thumb, later standardised to 45in, which was the width alnagers had to confirm before sealing a roll of cloth. The post was not finally abolished until 1699, by which time changes in fashion and the arrival of foreign imports resulted in too much confusion over cloth widths. Duty on cloth was finally abolished in 1724, but cloth seals continued throughout the1700s-1800s. By that time they were more likely to carry merchants' names or merchants' marks as personal guarantees of width and quality.

Thanks in part to English wool's renown for durability and fibre length, it sold all over the known world, taking English cloth seals to such far-flung spots as Jamestown in Carolina, Botany Bay in New

The collection of 46 cloth, bag and bale seals depicted here includes a broad range of types and designs you might find on English fields and riverside foreshores.

Not to scale

Not to scale

South Wales, Antwerp in Belgium and Madrid in Spain. The world's seas and oceans also hold numerous examples, as witnessed by the hundreds of seals that divers have recovered when exploring sunken wrecks.

Archaeologists on land and underwater can often derive more information from a cloth seal than they can from a lost coin. With a hammered silver coin they get the monarch's name and perhaps a date thanks to a mint mark. With a cloth seal they can get the year (and thus the monarch's name) the name (or initials) of the alnager, the town or city where the cloth was sealed, the cloth's width, even (in some cases) an impression of the cloth's weave pressed into the surface of the lead. Add scratched notes, dates, initials on the back of the seal giving information about pieces of cloth cut from the roll to sell to customers, and we can begin to appreciate just how much information a single find of a once casually discarded object can bring.

Leaden closures did not end with the abolition of alnage duty. Right down to the early years of the 20th century bags, sacks, bales and other containers often carried attractively embossed seals in some form. Farm fields are rich hunting grounds for them because many sealed sacks of seeds and fertiliser were opened on the fields where they were used and their seals dropped on the plough soil. They added to about 500 years of seal throwaways - more than enough to attract collectors.

You may start out wishing to achieve no more than making sure you have not included a seal among your tokens and tallies. But you might find that seals have more appeal than you initially expected.

Not to scale

Group of Roman seals. Even from a distance of 2,000 years the imperial busts and the letters AVG suggest the hand of officialdom at work on the closures.

Not to scale

Chapter 13

Collecting, Researching & Cataloguing

More than three-quarters of all leaden tokens and tallies that change hands in Britain were initially found by metal detectorists and mudlarks. Nevertheless a lot of collectors are themselves detectorists and mudlarks who form impressive collections during local searches. The buying and selling market in the sort of pieces we have looked at throughout this book is supplied largely by finders whose numismatic interests veer in other directions.

The most popular selling route lies via eBay's internet auction site, with only a few leaden tokens and tallies, such as Roman *tesserae*, pricier medieval pewter pieces, scarce hop tokens, and pictorial leads in unusually good condition, finding their way to the trays of the limited number of coin dealers who currently include paranumismatic series in their stock.

Your choice if you intend to collect comes down at present to scouring conventional dealers' postal or internet lists and their trays at coin fairs; or buying a metal detector and learning the rudiments of the hobby; or honing your auction house skills with a few bids on eBay. I shall leave those choices to you and assume that you are reading this page after a few months of acquisition so that you now have some dozens of pieces before you, and you are wondering where to go from here. Without hesitation my answer urges you to become involved with local research if you have managed to obtain some local pieces with initials and other possible clues to original ownership. Sifting through parish records, recording the names and trades of everyone who lived in the neighbourhood, parish or village 200 (perhaps more) years ago will totally absorb you. Find out if there are farms in the area still in the hands of families who have inhabited the district for generations. Old agricultural buildings might record the initials of original owners or builders (look above doors and windows). If you strike lucky and encounter a descendant I can promise you'll have an eager collaborator on further research as soon as you show him/her an initialled token or tally.

Another productive source of information is the oldest local cemetery, usually adjoining the parish church. Unworn gravestones will provide a wealth of local names. If any initials match those found on leaden tokens try a search of the Genuki website, a genealogist's playground where you can become heavily involved in the history of your parish - with much of the hard work probably already done by people who visited the site before you and added what they learned to the existing records. It can sweep you along like an unravelling detective story as you delve further and further into the village's past.

Your research should include making lists of all old farm names, as well as the areas of land they occupied; listing all local inns, blacksmith's premises and trades and crafts such as clockmaker or shoemaker that might have served the locality in pre-Victorian times. Perhaps there was an ecclesiastical establishment in your neighbourhood - an abbey, grange, or similar enterprise. The local Catholic priest might have much to tell you. And the local archaeological records should inform you of any leaden token or tally finds (medieval or earlier) made when excavations took place.

A couple of months on research will make you a very knowledgeable amateur historian. You should certainly have enough interesting facts to persuade the editor of your local newspaper that you could write an entertaining and informative feature about people from your neighbourhood's past. Show the editor your leaden finds so far. Make sure the paper

A wealth of information about people who lived and worked in your locality as far back as 1700 can be read on the headstones in the oldest graveyard in the parish. Their names, initials, trades and merchant marks can often be found carved into the old stones.

gets photographs of them. When printed they may jog the memories of readers who can tell you more, or who found something similar while digging their gardens.

Your county library, or even a local coin collectors' club if you enjoy such a luxury, may have copies of catalogues listing issues of 17th century copper token halfpennies. Try to make a record of all issuers for several miles around your home area. Some traders may also have issued lead tokens before moving on to copper. Study the illustrations carefully - the names of issuers, and especially any trade symbols and guild emblems recorded on the copper pieces. One day you might turn up a lead piece with similar markings.

Research never ends; it expands because your frustration at not finding answers you hoped for leads to widening the net. Before long you will have progressed from a local researcher to a county-wide researcher, hopefully finding more answers rather than more frustration. I shall leave you to decide how far to take matters as I move on to the question of cataloguing or otherwise recording your collection as it expands.

I feel confident that leaden token and tally collecting will develop as a result of this book's publication; also that many readers will devise their own excellent systems for recording finds. However, I wholeheartedly support the view that we also (perhaps only) need a system of classifying finds that is universally agreed between collectors so that we can communicate and refer clearly and unambiguously to a particular piece.

Conventional coin collectors have their catalogues; we need ours. I'm a fan of the system under development by paranumismatist and leaden token and tally enthusiast, David Powell. It is familiar to readers of *The Leaden Tokens Telegraph,* which is the newsletter I have edited and published (as an internet .pdf file) during the research and writing stages of this book. Each month contributor David Powell has illustrated one of the 32 types in his system with several clear illustrations depicting minor variations and associated design features within that type. As this book goes to press he has reached Type 7, with 25 types to go. Back issues of *The Leaden Tokens Telegraph* can be viewed on several internet sites. (Simply do a search on Google and type the words *Leaden Tokens Telegraph* into the address bar. You will be offered a wide choice of places to view issues from past and forthcoming months. There is no charge.)

As a foretaste I offer in the illustrations accompanying this chapter a simplified layout of the Powell System, showing just one example from each of the 32 categories. Explanatory notes on each of the 32 types follows this.

The Powell 32-Type Classification System For Leaden Tokens & Tallies

Type 1. Petalled flower. Apart possibly from Type 2, the commonest type. The number of petals varies between three and six, five or six being the most. Occasional pieces, usually larger, have the petals superimposed on a second design.

Type 2. Initials. Includes faces where the initials are dominant or equivalent in prominence with any ornamentation. Faces where small initials flank the main design will be classified according to that design. Items with both initials and numbers will be dealt with either here or under Type 8, depending on which is predominant, although it is recognized that they are hybrids.

Type 3. Segments. Includes any face consisting of three or more segments emanating from the centre, except that quartered designs classify:

a. under Type 12 if they have any regular design other than crosses and pellets.

b. under Type 14 if they are simple crosses, or crosses with pellets in the centre of the quarters, ie pseudo-medieval pennies.

c. remain here if they are cartwheel type pieces with the pellets near the perimeter (ie are not intended to imitate the medieval penny).

Type 4. Lis. A wide family of this designs, which includes also those faces where the outer components of the lis curve out so far as to be occasionally mistaken for the initials CC, the second C retrograde.

Type 5. Anchor. Fairly non-controversial.

Type 6. Ship. Fairly non-controversial.

Type 7. Hatching. Includes those faces where the entire surface is hatched in an identical manner; where the hatching is quartered, it becomes Type 12.

Type 8. Numerals. Some of these are probably hop tokens, and a pseudo-weight has been seen. In addition to faces with low numbers indicating a specific value, those with dates and nothing else come under this category.

Type 9. Irregular geometrical. This type accommodates a large number of abstract designs which do not fit into either Type 3 or Type 12, other than those which have an obvious circular theme, which are Type 31.

Type 10. Heads. Most of these are pseudo-coin designs which mimic the obverses of major series, (ie Edward I pennies), although that is not invariably so. Pieces which mimic Cantian Celtic, Roman or other ancients are also occasionally seen. Whole bodies, rather than heads, are Type 32.

Type 11. Tavern utensils. Bottles, jugs etc

Type 12. Squared geometric. Any quartered design where the number of segments is necessarily four, except:

a. Simple cartwheels - Type 3 as previously discussed.

b. Potential mill sails - Type 22.

Pieces with four quarters containing alternate horizontal and vertical lines will remain here for the moment, notwithstanding that they may depict millstones and should correctly reside in Type 22.

Type 13. Frameworks. This accommodates a number of designs which border between the abstract and the real, and which may actually represent objects, the nature of which cannot be determined. The design does not cover the whole face, or at least not without significant variation; if it did, it would belong to Type 9.

Type 14. Crosses. Not necessarily religious, although it might be. The cross should not obviously be the single letter X; if it is, the piece belongs in Type 2; otherwise, any design, abstract or real, which:

a. depicts two crossed lines or objects only as the major device, or

b. indicates by the central positioning of any pellets within the quarters of a cross that it is meant to simulate the medieval penny.

Type 15. Religious. Anything which is known to have religious use or depicts religious symbolism, (ie a crosier), apart from simple crosses covered by Type 14 above.

Type 16. Arms. Anything where the major type is a shield depicting heraldry.

Type 17. Trees and Plants. Anything botanical except national symbols, (ie the rose covered by Type 25).

Type 18. Birds. Any birds except national symbols, (ie the eagle covered by Type 25).

Type 19. Animals. Self explanatory. Same proviso as per the last two types.

Type 20. Merchant marks. Usually monograms, these were frequently used by the more prominent tradesmen until at least the late 17th century.

Type 21. Trade symbols and equipment. Accommodates faces containing the type of trade-related material which one might expect to find on the main series of 17th century tokens, with the one exception that anything related to milling goes in Type 22.

Type 22. Mills. Depictions of mills and designs likely to represent mill sails. Squared geometric designs which could be mill stones should probably go in here, but are being left in Type 12 because of the uncertainty. One interesting possibility: could some of the petals of Type 1, and/or the spoked wheels of Type 3, represent crude attempts to render mill wheels or sails?

Type 23. Buildings. Any buildings other than mills, which go in Type 22. Division into rustic, urban and military might be possible, but I have resisted the temptation to sub-classify.

Type 24. Obscure characters. Any characters that are not obviously letters (Type 2) or numbers (Type 8), although they may be crude attempts at one or the other.

Type 25. Miscellaneous objects, royal. Symbols such as crowns, roses, eagles and the like. The late Elizabethan pieces with double-headed eagle on one side and crowned rose on the other, circa 1570-1600, are a notable example, although they are not part of the run of crude agricultural pieces.

Type 26. Miscellaneous objects, celestial. This contains such items as the sun, moon, and stars; also globes, although these could be a reference to a tavern or playhouse of such a name, rather than to the heavens. There were two total eclipses of the sun visible from England in 1715 and 1724, and it is conjectured that these may have been the inspiration for crescent and star types.

Type 27. Miscellaneous objects, secular. A catch-all for items which are clearly objects, whether identifiable or not, and which do not come into other categories such as Type 11 (tavern implements) or Type 16 (coats of arms).

Type 28. Outer rim series. Certain series exist which have an outer rim with various types of filler, (ie shading in). These could reasonable be sub-classified Type 28.nn, where nn indicates the classification of the subject matter of the inner part of the token according to the above scheme, which would take in certain series, such as some of the very small ecclesiastical tokens of the medieval period, which the main classification does not so easily cover.

Type 29. Words. Complete words or names are rare on lead tokens, but not unknown.

Type 30. Pellets. Accommodates pieces which have pellets and nothing else, as opposed to obscure blobs; the latter are unclassified until identified.

Type 31. Circular geometric. Another simplistic type; may or may not have a central hub.

Type 32. People. Anyone standing, sitting, riding, walking, running or lying down; in other words, anything which shows the whole person, rather than a mere head or bust. The latter go in Type 10.

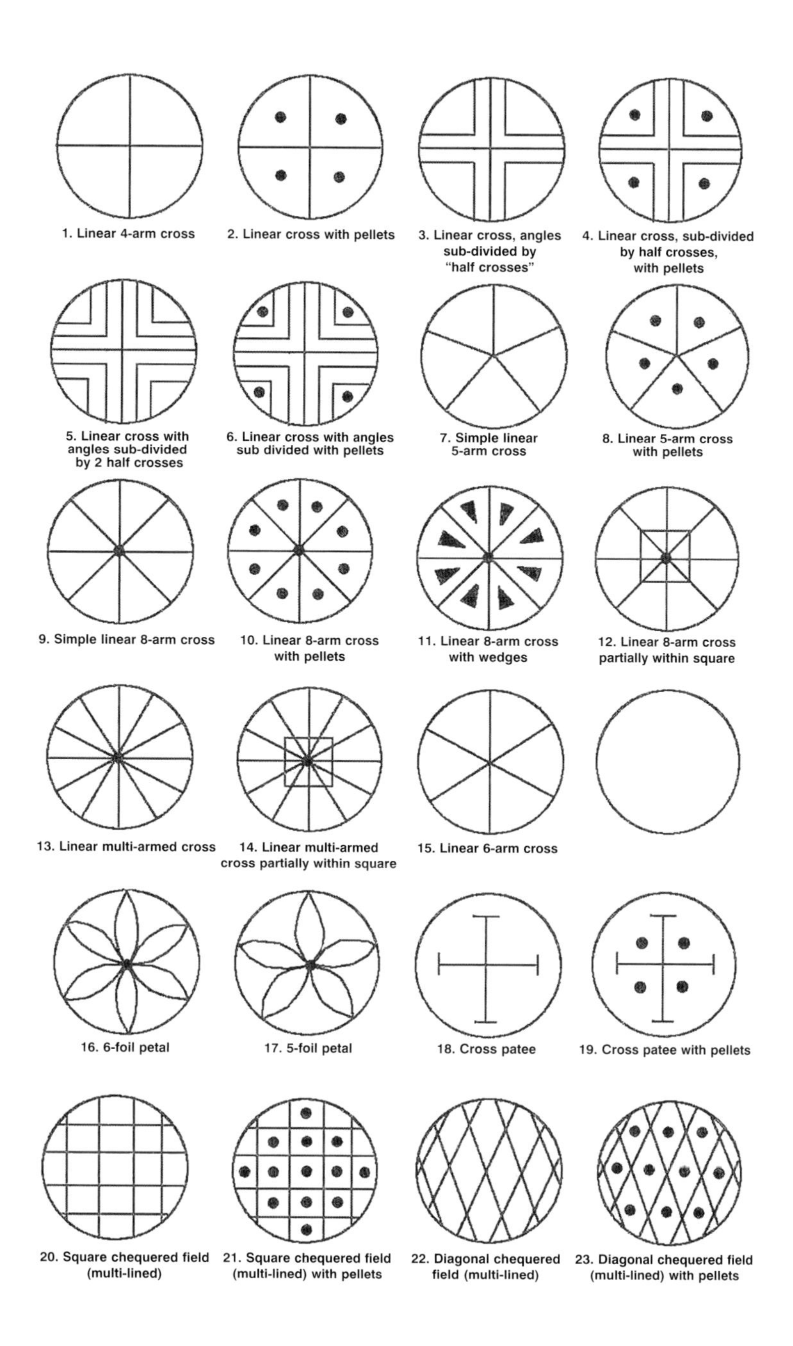

As I said previously, I'm sure many readers will devise their own excellent systems for recording finds. One reader of *The Leaden Tokens Telegraph* - Paul Baylis - has already done so, using neat line drawings and setting them out using an Excel layout. A couple of his pages are illustrated here to show readers what can be achieved with a little care and a lot of enthusiasm for our subject.

24. Anchor (various)
25. Multi-armed spiral cross
26. Cross patee over diaganol 4-armed cross
27. Farm gate (various)
28. Multi-stars/crosses
29. Plants/flowers
30. Stars and moon
31. Linear 7-armed cross with pellets
32. Crown
33. Shield (various)
34. Fleur de lis designs (ranging from standard form to vertical line accosted by crescent on either side) with or without pellets
35. Banded vertical cross
36. Circles
37. Multi-pellets
38. Boxed vertical cross
39. Star
40. Flower
41. Jug, bottle/glass
42. Cross fleury
43. Portcullis
44. Dividers

45. Bird
46. Trident
47. Heart
48. Linear
49.
50. Boat
51. Chevrons
52. 4-foil petal
53. Bell or mortar
54. Box within box
55. Line and two pellets
56. Linear cross with circle(s)
57. Petals with circle(s)
58. Bust
59. Vertical line with 2 or more horizontals
60. Cross with various hatched quarters
61. Open cross rounded corners
62. "Cog"
63. Hatching within circle(s)
64. Multi (terminated) armed cross
65. Multi-armed cross within box with border loops
66. Random hatching
67. Animal(s)
68. Multi-foil petal

Chapter 14

Some Puzzling Pieces

You are nearing the end of what is, I believe, the first book to discuss leaden tokens and tallies in a broad, introductory manner. I do hope it paves the way for other enthusiasts who will wish to concentrate in greater detail on narrower aspects of the subject. I can't think of any series, or associated series, within paranumismatics that offers greater scope for further detective work.

Who, I wonder, will unearth the answer to those puzzling petal types? They have come to light across England and France - the design replicated in every century from the 13th to the 19th - and have been found on riversides, arable land and during archaeological excavations in urban areas. But the symbolic meaning of the petals remains a mystery. Were they religious or secular? Did they serve as early communion tokens or token farthings in busy markets? Or were petals a secret sign of membership of some guild or group now unknown to us? When a reader comes up with the answer I shall welcome enlightenment.

The simple grid design found on numerous pieces that come from arable fields also merits thorough investigation. I like to think of the grid as a representation of an early agricultural harrow, and the leaden finds as tallies recording the harrowing that must have taken place once a year over many centuries as part of the agricultural cycle. But an alternative explanation - that these pieces have some connection with the game of chequers said to have been a favourite of mule drivers working packhorse routes - merits consideration. Taverns and inns named Chequers often flanked those ancient lines of communication.

Fleur-de-lis designs also occur far more often on English fields than one would expect to see them. The lis was a common enough symbol in early medieval England when cross-Channel links between state and ecclesiastical authorities were very close. But why should the lis continue to appear on so many leaden pieces long after the English monarchy and the English church had severed connections with France? Or are many pieces that we presently assign to the 17th and later centuries in fact much older?

Use of leaden pieces as fractional coinage cries out for further investigation. Is there a link between the many images seen on tokens and tallies and the similarly numerous designs on the foreign coins that must have changed hands in medieval market-places when Continental black money circulated in England? Poor people endured at least a thousand years' perpetual shortage of small change. We know that they halved and quartered silver pennies. Did they also make leaden pieces depicting parts of the designs and the mintmarks on current coins of the realm, adding leaden versions of black money when need arose? Close study of low denomination foreign coins of the 13th to 18th centuries, perhaps by Continental buyers of this book, will, I'm sure, shed much light on English monetary history.

Closer to home, I hope somebody discovers an early metal press once used to produce leaden tokens and tallies. And I'm itching to see more leaden finds from the north and west of England where grass fields abound and relatively few detectorists venture. Surely places such as Lancashire, Cumbria, West Durham, North Wales and Cornwall, where lead ore went hand-in-hand with poverty and the need for small change, must have produced numerous pieces that have yet to see the light of day since their accidental loss?

Yes, there is much more to be written. Please let me hear of it on publication.

The ubiquitous yet enigmatic petal design, in widespread use for more than a thousand years on both sides of the Channel. Does anyone now know what it signified?

This type of harrow was dragged across stubble and other previous crop remains to break them up and help to fertilize and prepare the ground for the next crop.

Not to scale

Were the men who did the work given tallies like these to record amounts of harrowing completed?

Almost as popular as petals, the fleur-de-lis decorated large numbers of English tokens and tallies. If we are correct on dating the finds, why did the design endure so long?

Not to scale

Black money like these examples circulated ubiquitously in England for centuries.

Leaden attempts to increase the numbers of long-cross pennies in circulation.

What was the method of manufacture for these well-made pieces?

Not to scale

Notes

Sources Consulted

Communion Tokens: Their History And Use,	Mary M. Tenney
Leaden Tesserae Of Rome And Its Environs,	M.I. Rostovtzeff
Money & Its Use In Medieval Europe,	P. Spufford
Nouveau Manuel De Numismsatique Du Moyen Age Et Moderne,	J.A. Blanchet
Plumbeis Antiquorum Numismatibus,	F. Ficorinii
Salisbury Museum Medieval Catalogue,	P. Saunders (Ed)
The Leaden Token-Coinage Of Egypt Under The Romans,	J.G. Milne
Une Histoire Économique Et Populaire Du Moyen Age: Les Jetons Et Les Méreaux	J. Labrot, et J. Henckes
A Descriptive Catalogue Of London Traders, Tavern & Coffee House Tokens Current In The 17th Century	J.H. Burn